We Happy WASPs

We Happy WASPs

Virginia in the Days of Jim Crow and Harry Byrd

by
Parke Rouse, Jr.

Dietz Press, Richmond, Virginia

Printed in the United States of America

ISBN: 0-87517-091-9

Design by Stinely Associates

For my own
particular Richmond WASP,
Betsy Gayle Rouse

Contents

The Virginian of the present time has ingrained in his character the cordial instincts, and the spirit of courtesy and hospitality which marked his ancestors. He has the English preference for the life of the country to the life of the city; loves horses and dogs, breeds of cattle, the sport of fox-hunting, wood-fires, Christmas festivities, the society of old neighbors, political discussions, traditions of this or that local celebrity, and to entertain everybody to the extent of, and even beyond, his limited means.

Many of these proclivities have been laughed at, and the people have been criticized as provincial and narrow-minded; but after all it is good to love one's native soil, and to cherish the home traditions which gave character to a race. Of the Virginians it may be said that they have objected in all times to being rubbed down to a uniformity with all the rest of the world, and that they have generally retained the traits which characterized their ancestors.

John Esten Cooke, 1883

Introduction

THIS BOOK is about three years I spent in Richmond—from 1940 through 1942—as a reporter for the *Richmond Times-Dispatch*. I had graduated from college in 1937, and served three years on the Newport News *Times-Herald*, my hometown afternoon paper. I was 25 when I moved to Richmond, and I knew it wouldn't be long before I went to war. Hitler had just invaded Poland, and the United States would join in two years later, after Japan had bombed Pearl Harbor on December 7, 1941.

This book is also about the social revolution under way in the United States in the 1940s. It had begun with Franklin D. Roosevelt's inauguration in 1933, and it continued through the Roosevelt and Truman presidencies, especially after the Supreme Court in 1954 ruled that public segregation of white and black students in public schools must cease.

But despite these disturbing issues, I found Richmond a delightful city. It was charmingly old-fashioned, with a strong Confederate spirit. It enjoyed an alert, intelligent leadership, especially in its two newspapers. In fact, it was they that attracted me to Richmond. In a South that seemed mired in racial issues, the Richmond papers seemed to offer hope.

~ ~ ~

In recent years, after I left Richmond to live in Williamsburg, a young friend named John Alexander came home during his freshman year at Wesleyan University in Connecticut and shocked us all. He said that he'd learned that we Virginians were WASPs.

"WASPs?," I asked. "What's a WASP? Is it good or bad?"

"It means we are White Anglo-Saxon Protestants," he said. He had learned it from his sociology professor, who believed that WASP dominance of the United States was coming to an end. Non-WASP minorities who had immigrated later to the United States were contesting the Anglo-Saxon Protestant leadership that began with Washington, Adams, Jefferson, Madison, and their mostly blue-eyed successors. Irish Catholics, blacks, Hispanics, and Orientals were knocking at the door.

It didn't take long to prove John Alexander right. In 1961 John Fitzgerald Kennedy was inaugurated as the first Catholic president of the United States. To me and most Americans, he certainly looked and sounded like a WASP, what with his Harvard degree and his cultivated speech. But Catholicism was only the beginning. Today we take variety of genders, skin colors, and faiths for granted.

I have written these memoirs to reveal a moment in the life of Virginia, perhaps the most Waspish state of the union. I hope it suggests a little of the civility, the fairness, and the tolerance that seem to me a part of the mixed legacy of Waspdom. Most of all, I hope it's as much fun to read as it was for me to recall.

1

Joining the *Times-Dispatch*

ON A FALL DAY IN 1940 I became a reporter for the *Richmond Times-Dispatch,* Virginia's largest newspaper. Another reporter showed me to my typewriter desk in the crowded city room of the two Richmond papers on Fourth Street. It was noon, and only a few staff members—editorial writers and women's department writers—were at work. The *Times-Dispatch* was a morning paper.

While I unpacked my dictionary and a few possessions, I heard the city editor call my name: "Rouse!" When I reached his table in the room's center he motioned me to sit down.

"I'm Frank McDermott," he said. "I'm your boss, and I want to tell you a few things."

Mac, as everyone called him, was a middle-aged man with rimless glasses and the physique of an ex-boxer. He seldom talked, but I found that he was easy to work for if you followed his instructions.

"I know you've been to college and worked for the Newport News papers, but I have to start you from scratch. It's for your best interest. You'll begin by writing obituaries, then go to the police beat to acquaint you with the layout of Richmond. After that—if you turn out all right—we'll fit you in where we need you. Any questions?"

Soon the city room began to buzz with reporters, who got their day's assignments from Mr. McDermott or from the state editor, Mr. Cottrell. By mid afternoon the room was jumping with reporters telephoning or heading out on the street to cover their beats—the State Capitol, city hall, courts, schools, or whatever. The *Times-Dispatch* prided itself on having a wider circulation than any other Virginia paper, including its afternoon counterpart, the *News Leader*. Both were good papers, occasionally cited by *Time* or *Newsweek* as leaders in America among dailies of 100,000 or so circulation.

Richmond Times-Dispatch

Obituaries are among journalism's worst chores. For weeks I spent my whole workday with my head in a strapped-on phone while I typed and edited the sad sagas of the day's deceased. Occasionally I got to write a front-page obituary, but even then I was not permitted to indulge in the Victorian euphemisms of my afternoon counterpart, Robert Munford, the *News Leader's* elderly obituarist. Bob was a portly bachelor who knew Richmond's bloodlines like the Prayer Book, and he used fulsome phrases like "one of this city's oldest and most distinguished families." Upper-crust Richmonders promised Bob to die in the morning so his paper would get first crack at their obit.

Old timers craved nothing more than a splendid Bob Munford obituary–except perhaps that their sons and daughters should marry old money. Richmond money.

I had arrived in Richmond by the C&O train from Newport News, a nervous 25-year-old, getting off at Main Street station and walking uphill on Main Street to the newspaper. The train trip was only 80 miles, but Richmond was a different world from Newport News, where I'd grown up. Richmond was old, historic, rich, and culturally resplendent. Newport News was a raw shipbuilding town, only 54 years old in 1940–a town where leading businessmen ate lunch at Woolworth's lunch counter.

Richmond's Main Street Station provided C&O connections to Newport News and westward to the Great Lakes.

Library of Virginia

In Richmond the strong smell of sweet-scented tobacco wafted up from the cigarette plants that lined lower Main Street, called "Tobacco Road," along the old James River Canal, and excited my emotions like incense.

But what attracted me most about Richmond was the newfound progressivism of the *Times-Dispatch* under its young editor, Virginius Dabney, and managing editor, Leon Dure. Both the *Dispatch* and the *News Leader* had once been owned by Richmond's Bryan family, but the Bryans had sold the *Times-Dispatch* in 1914. Then, in the 1930s, a skilled Georgia publisher named Mark Etheridge had revived the dormant *Times-Dispatch,* imbuing it with fresh ideas and some of the zest of Roosevelt's New Deal. Along with Ralph McGill's Atlanta *Constitution* and a few other Southern dailies, the paper had begun to stand out for its editorials urging fairer treatment of blacks. Virginia needed the new voice.

To forego the *Times-Dispatch*'s competition, the Bryans in 1940 bought back the *Times-Dispatch* and housed it with the *News Leader* in their building on Fourth Street. Then, to replace Mark Etheridge, who had been lured from Richmond to manage the *Louisville Times* and *Courier-Journal* for Barry Bingham, Publisher John Stewart Bryan hired John Dana Wise of South Carolina as publisher of both his papers. When I arrived in Richmond in 1940, Bryan's son Tennant was just going into wartime Navy service, and Jack Wise was running the papers. The elder Bryan had absented himself to serve as president of the College of William and Mary.

As I lugged my suitcase up Main Street, I caught glimpses of the James River on my left, hidden mostly by Victorian storefronts of banks, brokerages, and insurance offices. This was Richmond's Wall Street, most of it burned down in 1865 when Robert E. Lee's Confederate army, evacuating Richmond to escape Grant, had set fire to Confederate supplies to keep them from the enemy. Alas, the fire destroyed most of downtown Richmond, then a metropolis of 40,000.

To my right as I climbed Main, I got glimpses of Capital Square and of the classical Capitol which Jefferson had copied in the 1780s from a Roman temple in Nimes, France. Once the Capitol had offered a view of the James and the opposite shore of Manchester (now part of Richmond), but commerce now obstructs the view. One Main Street store which caught my eye was the B. T. Crump Company, displaying a life-size white horse in its window to advertise saddlery. Main Street still evoked horse-and-buggy Virginia.

In the autumn heat the tarred streets oozed under the sun. On side streets I saw the purple blossoms of paulonia trees, canopied over by wisteria. And in the heat I heard the siren song of cicadas, overridden at times on residential streets by the cry of the ice man, "I-c-c-c-c-c-c-e Man" or of the fish man, "F-e-e-e-e-s-s-s-h Man." I could tell I would like Richmond.

When I turned onto Fourth Street to the newspaper I was

Author's Collection

Virginia's Capitol, designed in part by Jefferson, looks over Main Street and the James River. The Virginia General Assembly met surprised to find two handsome Victorian houses that had survived the westward sweep of downtown commerce. One was the art gallery of William Young, at whose show window I was often to stop and admire the paintings. (Alas, they never came within a reporter's income.) And across Franklin Street from Young's was the brick house of the charming elderly widow, Mrs. R. Carter Scott, whose magnolia tree and wrought-iron fence were remnants of the horse-drawn age, just disappearing. Both Mrs. Scott's house and Mr. Young's shop in the 1950s were to go the way of urban progress, torn down to make way for parking lots. To me they evoked the graceful past.

~ ~ ~

Many of the *Times-Dispatch* staff seemed as old as Methuselah, for in those early Social Security days many people had to work into their 70s for lack of retirement money. Bob Golden was a bright-eyed old gaffer who could still dash out a breezy column. Mr. Cottrell, the state editor, had a walrus mustache and wore his felt hat at work. Unsmiling Allyn Tunis, who ran the Sunday editorial section, had written books with his sister, Edith Tunis Sale.

Across the way, in the *News Leader* city room, I got to know Bill Christian, the managing editor, and Charlie Hamilton, city editor. Others who came to be friends were Isabel Ziegler, Dolores Lescure, and Sylvia Costen, women's editors, and Roy Flanagan and Mike Houston, who had several books to his credit. I saw them most often in the Greasy Spoon, the noisy restaurant next door to the paper, where we sometimes gobbled down a meal.

~ ~ ~

Thanks to the fame of editors Douglas Freeman and Virginius Dabney, the *News Leader* and the *Times-Dispatch* attract-

C. Herron

Virginius Dabney was the editor of the Times-Dispatch *and a Southern leader in the movement in the 1940s to treat blacks more fairly.*

ed excellent talent from colleges and from other papers. When I arrived I found the veteran reporters George Prince Arnold and Jim Latimer covering the Capitol, Overton Jones the city hall, Maurice Dean the federal courts, and Frank Eleazer, Whitton Morse, Cooper Etheridge, and others on general assignment. The best feature writer was Paul Saunier, who traveled the hinterland to uncover odd rural characters. He sought Thoreau-like figures who marched to a different drum—or no drum at all. In those days he found these in rural Virginia.

Paul was especially attracted by a lady named Birdie May Baugh, who wrote saccharin letters to the paper from her home in Belona, Virginia. She was absorbed in bird lore and lovingly described the patrons of her bird-feeder by species and name, following their antics like a doting parent. Eventually Paul went to Belona and interviewed Birdie May, who proved well worth it.

A typical Birdie May letter was this:

> . . . Yesterday I was made very anxious about Dickie Mockingbird as he did not put in an appearance at the feeding station bath at all. I saw him many times Friday, when he ate raisins and then quenched his thirst. After it stopped snowing I called him repeatedly, put out raisins,

and poured hot water in the baths. But Dickie failed to show up and I became alarmed.

This morning he appeared about 8:30, and devoured many raisins. I wish he could explain his absence. Dickie drove such a pretty blue jay away from my front porch a few days ago. He is not at all hospitable . . .

The *Times-Dispatch* gave space to many subjects, like its continuing editorial controversy with the *Raleigh News and Observer* over which state had the most skunks. And there were endless letters about the relative virtues of spoon bread, batter bread, and egg bread. People had time to read and to write to the editor.

~ ~ ~

Gradually I got to know all the staff—even the women who wrote about engagements and weddings. Society Editor Corbin Old lived in the Chesterfield Apartments ("For the newly wed and the nearly dead") and wore her hat at work. When I asked why, she said "Because I'm a *lady* and not used to working. If you weren't from Newport News you'd know that." When I submitted to her the engagement announcement of an admiral's daughter, she was unenthusiastic. "Admirals may be big stuff in Newport News," she told me, "but if they don't live in Richmond, we don't give them much space."

When Colonel William Royall (he had fought Virginia's last duel) died at his apartment in the Chesterfield, near Corbin's, she made a condolence call on his daughters and found them drinking sherry and eating beaten biscuits over his remains. "Looked just like he did in life," she told me, offhandedly. "His coat was covered with tears and biscuit crumbs."

As a $35-a-week reporter, I couldn't afford a car, so I stayed at a boarding house on nearby Monument Avenue, with a view from my window of Jefferson Davis's statue. Each morning I walked to work at the paper, passing Lee's statue (facing south to hearten Confederates) and J. E. B. Stuart's (facing north to defy Yankees). The churches on Monument and its connecting Franklin Street fascinated me: All Saints Episcopal, later torn down when the congregation moved to River Road; Beth Ahabah Synagogue and its scholarly Rabbi Edward Calisch; and St. James' Episcopal with its popular rector, Churchill Gibson.

Franklin Street, I concluded, was Richmond's Fifth Avenue, with classy stores at one end and old mansions at the other. Many of the houses since those days have given way to apartments, offices, and clubs. But once Franklin Street had sheltered most of Richmond's first families, including the Chiswell Dabney Langhornes and their beautiful daughters, led by Nancy, who became Lady Astor.

One Richmonder I knew, Beverley Bland Munford, liked to tick off the names of the Franklin Street families he had known, from Monroe Park east to the *Times-Dispatch* office. "I don't want to know any more people than I know now," he liked to say. "I have more friends than I can keep up with. I wish Richmond would stay the way it was in World War I."

Ambling to work each morning and bumping home by trolley at night, I grew familiar with the reminders I saw of Richmond's many wars and of its ex-residents: John Marshall, Henry Clay, Edgar Allan Poe, Bojangles Robinson. I would have liked to write about them. But all those hopes ended when I got to my desk at the paper and strapped on my telephone headset to spend the day talking to undertakers.

~ ~ ~

"Rouse!"

It was Mr. McDermott. I hustled to his desk.

"Rouse, you've done obits long enough now. Beginning tonight I'm putting you on the police beat with Red McCalley."

That night Red and I set out in a company car equipped with a police radio to follow the cryptic calls that signaled trouble. Each offense was designated by a number, to which the broadcaster added the address of the offense. At least it was more exciting than obits.

Red had been on the police beat a long time and knew all the policemen, detectives, and complaints. He was a moody Irishman with reddish hair and complexion, and he was impressed that I'd been to college. We would start each night by checking at each police station, meanwhile following up any call that seemed to promise a news story.

Recognizing one call as a peeping Tom, Red drove close to the scene, parked, and led me down alleys quietly till we came upon the police. They were dividing their attention between a beautiful young woman who was undressing before an open window and a young man who crouched in the alley watching her. When the police grabbed the peeping Tom, Red tried to persuade them to let him off. "That woman *wanted* him to see her," he argued.

It was on the police beat that I saw death for the first time. It was a gruesome sight. Hearing a homicide call on the police radio, I dashed to the Hotel John Marshall and followed the police up the elevator to the room of an elderly salesman, who lay dead on the floor. He had had a heart attack and died reaching for his nitroglycerine. Another night I responded to a homicide call at the John Marshall to find that an elderly Newport News friend of mine had jumped from the roof and killed himself. He had just been discharged from Tucker's Sanatorium and had asked his family to stop and let him use the hotel restroom en route to Newport News. He was depressed that he was going blind and he could no longer work.

~ ~ ~

One night Red took me to Scott's Addition, near "the wrong side" of Broad Street. It was the "wrong side" because saloons had been permitted on that side in pre-Prohibition days, and ladies were unwelcome there. The building we entered was labeled Richmond Willow Works, and we walked upstairs to find ourselves in what was apparently a bordello. "I want you to meet Hortense Blair," Red told me as we entered.

Author's Collection

Political cartoons by Fred Seibel strengthened the editorial policies of the Times-Dispatch *during the years of civil rights debate.*

We sat down amid a room full of uncomfortable looking soldiers. Then Hortense came in. She was a short old woman in a pale blue evening dress, and she made a great to-do over us. When I stood up at her entrance, she slapped her fat knees and laughed, "Look at that boy stand up! Ain't no man stood up for me in a long time!" She sat down to talk with us, offering us beer or Coca Colas. "Where you been, Red? I've missed you." She ignored the rest of the room.

Red told her I'd wondered if she were any kin to the Reverend John Durburrow Blair, Richmond's first Presbyterian preacher, back in colonial times.

"Oh, yeah," she said, "I'm kin to all them rich Blairs out in the West End, but I'm the only one fool enough to work for a living."

Red explained that I would sometimes cover the police beat and would appreciate any news tips she might give me.

Virginia Historical Society

Main Street was the center of Richmond's highrise banks and brokerages, crowded in World War II with two-way traffic and trolley cars.

"Sure, sure," she said. "Anything he wants, but I may not be here long. Old Congressman Boykin is trying to run us out of here on account of Camp Lee. He's nothin' but an old fart-nosed ferret." She referred to a Democratic representative from South Carolina.

After Red and I finished up at the newspaper office at midnight, we would ride in his car to Chimborazo Hill, in east Richmond, and drink bourbon mixed with Chimborazo spring water. His real name was Chester Gray McCalley, and his mother, who lived on Chimborazo Hill, was president of the Cup of Cold Water Chapter of the Woman's Christian Temperance Union. "But that don't bother me," he sighed.

Sometimes Red and I joined one or two other reporters to relax over drinks and then a midnight supper at some restaurant. Virginia law then prohibited mixed drinks in public places, so one of us had to sneak a bottle in, against the law. Among the restaurants that winked at such "brown-bagging" was the Hotel William Byrd Coffee Shop on Broad Street.

One night our group phoned a local bootlegger to bring us a bottle to a rear booth of the coffee shop. Just as the bourbon arrived, two plainclothes cops with sidearms sprang from adjoining booths and grabbed the bourbon, the bootlegger, and a stack of dollar bills we'd ante'd up to pay for it. Then the cops took our names and summoned us to City Hall next day to pay fines or face trial. What was worse, the *Times-Dispatch* police log listed our violation next day and gave our names. I hoped my parents never saw it.

But it all gave me a sense of Richmond's infinite variety. I was on my own in the big city. Who knew where it would end?

2

Pearl Harbor Changes Life

ON SUNDAY, DECEMBER 7, 1941, my brother Randolph, a recently commissioned Navy ensign, was driving me from Newport News back to Richmond after a weekend with our parents. Just as we were passing the entrance to Camp Peary, the music on the car radio was interrupted.

"National alert! The Japanese are bombing Pearl Harbor!"

We listened in fury to the account of the dawn air strike which had hit the Pacific naval base and was destroying so many lives and battleships. Never had I been so shocked.

I was the eldest of four boys, all of military age. Two of my brothers were in uniform, one in the Army and the other in the Navy. My parents lived in fear that all of us would soon be at war. Listening to the story of Pearl Harbor, I realized at once that it had changed life for all Americans. Now we would be totally at war.

When I got back to the *Times-Dispatch*, Mr. McDermott and the staff were grim. Virginia was a likely naval and air target for the Axis, especially for their submarines. Already German U-boats had attacked British and American ships off the Virginia capes. I knew that one German sub had been sunk off the North Carolina coast.

The *Times-Dispatch* and the *News Leader* fully supported President Roosevelt's help to Great Britain and France in the months before Pearl Harbor. Now the paper sent me to Puerto Rico to write about joint Army-Navy amphibious exercises at Vieques Beach in preparation for America's entry into combat.

As a member of the Senate's Armed Forces Committee, Virginia's senior senator, Harry Byrd, was also in Puerto Rico to observe the landings. After a day on the invasion beach, I sat with the Senator and our Army and Navy hosts one night in an outdoor pavilion while Puerto Rico's governor, Rexford Guy Tugwell, entertained us at drinks and dinner. Meanwhile a few perfumed dance hall hostesses slipped into the pavilion, looking for free drinks and pickups. Approaching the glacial Senator, one senorita cooed, "Please, meestah, will you buy me a drink?" He looked at her as if she were crazy.

"Go away, young woman," Byrd barked. The senorita saw he meant it and moved on to other prey.

Soon afterward I spent a hectic night driving from Richmond to Newport News and back with photographer Frank Dementi to cover some Italian crewmen's sabotage of three of their ships, which happened to be in the harbor there. Il Duce's Italy had declared war against Great Britain and France, joining Hitler's forces. Then the Coast Guard promptly followed President Roosevelt's orders to seize all Italian ships in American waters as violators of American neutrality. The crews of the Italian merchant men immediately destroyed their engines and navigational equipment, before the Coast Guard had time to strike. Dementi, a wild Italian himself, drove 90 miles an hour with me to Newport News and back to make the paper's deadline. The story and pictures made front page.

Virginia Historical Society

Douglas Freeman works in the office at his early home in Byrd Park. A preacher as well as biographer, he broadcast inspirational talks.

Soon after I joined the *Times-Dispatch* I had a note from Douglas Freeman, editor of the *News Leader,* inviting me to his office. My great-uncle had served with him on the board of the University of Richmond, and "the Doctor," as everyone called him, wanted to welcome me to Richmond. In his office above our newsroom he worked beneath a quotation from antiquity, "Time alone is irreplacable; waste it not." I noticed that the key word "irreplacable" was misspelled. The sign was the Doctor's way of telling visitors to make it snappy. He moved at a rapid pace, but he never seemed hurried.

Dr. Freeman had just published his four-volume *R. E. Lee* in 1934–35 and was well into his *Lee's Lieutenants.* He was a rare combination of scholar and journalist, and in wartime he also became Virginia's military oracle. Twice daily on weekdays he delivered his eloquent, unscripted newscasts over WRNL microphones in his office or his bedroom study at home. He simplified wartime logistics by likening European localities to Virginia's: "The army must travel from Cherbourg to Paris, a trip like that from Norfolk to Richmond," he would say.

He was also a student of languages and loved rendering sonorous words like "Ben-GOZZ-i" or "Wal-HALL-a" or "Bee-ZAHR-tay," or "EEL DOO-chay" or "VAHR-macht." The Army and Navy War Colleges constantly called on him to lecture their top-ranking officers. He was an expert on military strategy.

To accomplish his daily routine as editor, newscaster, and biographer, Dr. Freeman gradually reduced his night's sleep from eight hours to six. This he supplemented by a catnap at home after he'd worked at the newspaper from 3:30 A.M. to 12:30, had written his editorials, answered his mail, kept his appointments with staff members and visitors, and made two newscasts. After the afternoon nap, he worked on his biography until he dined with his family and then retired early.

Life magazine sent staffers to Richmond to record the Doc's

Newport News Daily Press

Salvador Dali was an intense artist with bright eyes and curling mustache who amused Americans during World War II with his eccentricities.

2:30 A.M. wake-up, his drive in darkness from his home–first on Richmond's Boulevard and later from Westhampton–down Monument Avenue to salute the statue of Lee astride Traveler. Arriving at his office, he breezed through newspapers and Associated Press wire copy, tapped out his editorials, and by breakfast time was reassuring Richmond that God still reigned.

Dr. Freeman's calm disposal of world complexities somehow made life easier for his hearers. When Governor James H. Price in the 1940s created a wartime state defense network, he inevitably asked Dr. Freeman to head it. Under the Doctor, every Virginia locality developed plans for food and gas rationing, and for bomb shelters in case of attack.

Of all the people I've met in life, Douglas Freeman was the most memorable. He and Virginius Dabney became my lifetime friends and mentors.

The war in 1940–41 moved steadily closer to Virginia. One day the *Times-Dispatch* sent me to Caroline County with photographer Joe Colognori to interview and photograph Salvador Dali and his wife, Gala, who had just moved to Virginia to escape the war in Europe. They were house guests of a wealthy American expatriate from Paris, Caresse Crosby, who had rented the DeJarnette family plantation, Hampton Manor, near Bowling Green, to accommodate her friends. Caresse had been an owner of the Parisian bookstore, Shakespeare and Company, which published James Joyce.

Caresse wanted Dali and her other guests to continue to create their paintings and books in peaceful Virginia, undisturbed by the war, but I'm afraid my *Times-Dispatch* story tipped off the media to a story none of them could ignore. When photographer Joe Colognori and I reached the plantation, we found a Jeffersonian mansion full of beautiful furniture and exotic artists. In a moment the immaculate Dali appeared, accompanied by Gala, who translated for him. (He understood English but was reluctant to speak it.) Both were

Richmond Newspapers

Hampton Manor, a DeJarnette plantation in Virginia, was home to Salvadore Dali and other aesthetes who fled Paris in the 1940s.

tiny, bird-like, and stylish. His wide mustache was rolled thin and waxed at the ends.

Julian McCarthy

Frank McCarthy served on General George Marshall's staff in World War II and then as Assistant Secretary of State. He later produced "Patton."

Through Gala, Dali told us he continued to paint despite interruptions from gallery-owners, designers, and interviewers like me. It was clear, though, that he welcomed publicity and would do anything to get it. For Joe Colognori's pictures, Dali had a farm hand lead a cow into the living room for photographs, treading on Oriental rugs and polished oak floors. Then the artist led us into the garden, where mannequins dressed in pastel bridesmaid's dresses floated about in canoes on a pond. Meanwhile a phonograph played Chopin waltzes. It was breathtaking.

My account of the Dalis, complete with cow and mannequins, occupied a prominent space in Sunday's *Dispatch,* and *Life* magazine immediately flew a writer and photographer to Bowling Green. The Dalis later left Virginia for New York, but Caroline County never ceased to talk about them, about Caresse, and about her freethinking friends.

~ ~ ~

One of Richmond's wartime heroes was Colonel Frank McCarthy, who was secretary to Army Chief of Staff General

George C. Marshall during the war and who later became Marshall's assistant secretary when the general became President Truman's Secretary of State. Serving in England at one point in the war and forbidden by British law to bring back to America his British currency, Frank phoned his widowed mother in Richmond's Fan District and invited her to fly to England and help spend it.

Lillian McCarthy at first liked the idea, but then she remembered her tomatoes.

"I can't, Frank," she finally said. "My tomahtoes (Virginians call them "tomahtoes," like the English) are beginning to ripen, and I can't bear to leave them."

Lillian's friends shared her pride in Frank and his younger brothers: Julian, who became a vice president of American Tobacco, and Billy, a banker. When Frank finally flew back to the United States and joined the State Department, he came to Richmond to visit his mother. One of Lillian's West Avenue neighbors, Helena Caperton, wrote to her son-in-law, Barry Bingham, who was in the Navy at Pearl Harbor: "All of Lillian's old friends have come to West Avenue to kiss the A.S.S." For propriety's sake she added "(Assistant Secretary of State.)"

Frank was a graduate of VMI and first made his name in the 1930s by helping with the Hollywood production of "Brother Rat," featuring a young actor named Ronald Reagan. That gave him a taste for celebrities and show business. After he retired from the State Department, he became a Hollywood producer and made "Patton."

Soldiers increased on Richmond's streets after Congress in September 1940 passed the draft act. Camp Lee on the eastern outskirts of Petersburg became a huge Army base, with other bases at Bellwood Arsenal and Byrd Airport.

One well educated serviceman from out of town was so turned off by Richmond's blandness that he composed a poetic indictment of the town's shortcomings. He sent it to a local radio gossip columnist, Agnes Moyler Jones, who each Tuesday broadcast a "What's New in Richmond" program over a local station, sponsored by Montaldo's fashion store. Agnes was never able to learn what peevish soul had written it:

Reflections
On Hearing Agnes Moyler Jones
On Her Tuesday Evening Radio Program

Lady, prone to talk and not to listen,
Would you make your program glisten,
Will that egg you're laying hatch?
Agnes, better start from scratch.

Just one man's opinion frank,
Neither enemy nor crank.
This advice may come adversely.
Still, I'll state my case, and tersely.

Strangers listening to your chatter
Know exactly what's the matter:
You must talk about a city
Neither gay, nor bright, nor pretty,
One whose natives' interests leading
Are but gossip, drink and breeding.

Though pathetic in your loyalty
To a threadbare, inbred "royalty,"
This is simply not enough, dear.
A few minutes of such stuff, dear,
Fills one with the deepest pity
For your sponsor. Heed this ditty.

Something do to make them wake up.
Give them one good rousing shake-up.

"I'll scratch your back, you scratch mine"
  Hardly makes a program fine.

Here's the truth now: Lots of folks
  Find Richmond full of bores and soaks,
Most pretentious, dull and dowdy,
  And its outlook pretty cloudy
Little culture lights its gloom,

  Stupidly, from birth to tomb,
Its natives plod. No decent club,
  Hotel, restaurant, or pub
Offers entertainment, cheer. Outside of the ABC,
  Little comfort will there be.

Newport News *Daily Press*

GIs and sailors on leave danced with local girls at USO headquarters in Richmond. Most servicemen were headed overseas from Virginia.

True, your task is monumental.
You must earn your keep and rental.
If Montaldo's doesn't like it,
If your "public" up and hike it,
You are trapped, nor can prevent it,
Nor a lively piece invent it.

Virginia Historical Society, courtesy Valentine Museum

Sailors and soldiers crowded Richmond on weekends in World War II. Here, on a Sunday morning, USO girls took servicemen to church.

Richmond's soirees, clods and hags,
Bottles clutched in paper bags,
Offer nothing. A reporter
Can say little that she orter.

[The paper bags were to hide the whiskey which club members had to take with them because of Virginia's restrictions at that time against the public serving of mixed drinks.]

Shallow, superficial, green,
Unread, lumpish, smug, and mean,
Backward, insular and sappy,
Blatant, bovine, and slap-happy
These, and compliments, please send
To your antique lady friend.

My New Year's wish–you may repeat it,
Indeed I pray you, don't delete it–
Is that your program, overripe,
Will never suffer dearth of tripe
My fervent resolution, mind,
Is goodbye, Richmond, and its kind.

One further thought is cheering, too.
You won't be seeing me, madame
Nor I be hearing you.

Poor Agnes Jones was crushed to think anybody could write so cruelly of Richmond or of her broadcast. She especially resented the characterization of Richmond society as "clods and hags, Bottles clutched in paper bags." But as she grew older and as more "new people" changed the city's character, I think she grew more reconciled to the rude critique. Most of us thought it came from some Harvard smartass.

Valentine Museum

Williams Dam west of Richmond was built to divert part of James River into a seven-mile canal around falls of the river to lower Richmond.

3

Caught Up In Politics

"ROUSE!"

It was nearly press time one January midnight, and I was clearing off my desk to go home.

When I got to Mr. McDermott's desk, he told me to sit down.

"George Arnold has been missing too many stories on Capitol Hill," he said without preliminary. "I want you to take over his beat beginning this afternoon to see how you do. Jim Latimer will show you the ropes."

I had been at the paper less than a year, and I hadn't dared to hope for such a good beat so soon. The paper's specialty was Virginia politics, especially when the General Assembly met from mid-January through March.

"What you've handled up to now has been simple," Mr. Mac

Newport News Daily Press

Bill Tuck, left, was lieutenant governor and Colgate Darden Jr. was governor from 1942 to 1946. Tuck succeeded Darden. Both were well-liked.

told me. "No competition except the Leader. But on the Hill you'll be up against the *Washington Post*, the *Virginian Pilot*, and the press services. It's dog eat dog."

"I know, sir, and I'll do my best," I mumbled.

"You've got to win the confidence of Governor Darden and the rest of them," he said. "Think you can do it?"

"You bet I can," I said.

I was embarrassed to face George Prince Arnold, for he was a veteran newspaperman of high reputation. He came from a family I knew in Waverly and lived at the Commonwealth Club, where he saw many movers and shakers of Virginia politics. In fact, when Jim Latimer had approached him about joining the newly-organized Richmond chapter of the Newspaper Guild, George had told him, "Jim, I belong to only three organizations in the world: the Episcopal church, the Democratic party, and the Commonwealth Club. That's all I want to."

I got to Capital Hill at a promising moment in Virginia politics. Colgate Darden, Jr., had just become governor, six weeks after Pearl Harbor, and the legislature was about to meet. Darden proved one of the ablest men ever to govern Virginia.

Youth is a time when you look for heroes, and Darden became one of mine. He was the ideal public servant–decisive, fair, even-tempered, and genuinely democratic. Though elected with the aid of Virginia's Byrd Democratic machine, he was pretty much his own man. Besides being a Norfolk lawyer, he was married to Constance duPont, daughter of Irenée duPont of Delaware, and the Dardens worked for and gave quietly to many good causes. Perhaps to offset his duPont connection, Colgate Darden was very down-to-earth. He drove his own car and was easily accessible to press and public. He'd graduated from the University of Virginia and attended Cambridge, and he read widely, with a critical mind and a sense of the ridiculous.

Darden made one mistake as governor, and it was a lulu. Without prior notice to Douglas Freeman, he announced after his inauguration that he was dissolving the statewide civil defense committees that Governor James Price had earlier created under Freeman's lead. "You can't fight a war with committees," Darden said in explanation.

After Dr. Freeman had responded the next day with a scathing *News Leader* editorial, Governor Darden recognized his mistake

Newport News *Daily Press*

At the heart of Virginia's WASP culture is George Washington's statue in Capitol Square, adjacent to the Capitol itself. In the background is the tower of St. Paul's Church.

in not meeting first with Dr. Freeman, and he publicly apologized.

~ ~ ~

Virginia's columned Capitol, built in 1785–88 on its hill overlooking the James, was the hub of Richmond's pre-Civil War business area, and it remains so. With its surrounding buildings, it forms a campus of ancient trees, statues, and oversexed squirrels. Although, unhappily, the tall offices have grown up to block the Capitol's view of the James, the ambience of Capitol Square is still striking. The scent of tobacco rises up from the Main Street cigarette factories, and the chimes of St. Paul's Church across the street ring the passing of each hour.

Flower vendors once lined sidewalks from the Capitol to the nearby Medical College of Virginia, selling bright bouquets at all seasons. And in my Richmond years, black jubilee singers occasionally sang on street corners for tips. One tune was "Gospel Train's A'Moverin," accompanied by syncopated movements of the singers, simulating the turning of locomotive wheels:

> Gospel train's a'moverin' . . .
> Get on bo'd, get on bo'd.
> Gospel train's a'moverin' . . .
> Choo-choo, choo-choo, choo-choo.

Another song that delighted street audiences had four stanzas, each ending "Gonna Jump on the Baptist Side." Each stanza held out the virtues of one denomination–Methodist, Episcopal, Presbyterian, and Holy and Sanctified. One of the four singers would start,

> "Methodist, Methodist is my name,
> Methodist till I die . . ."

Then the other would join in:

> "But when old death come a-runnin' after me . . . "

(other voices joining):

> "Gonna JUMP on de Baptist side!"

The point of the song was that the literal, Bible-based credo of Southern Baptists appeals to blacks. As one minister put it, "If you find a black who isn't a Baptist, somebody's been fooling with him."

~ ~ ~

When the General Assembly came to town for six weeks, beginning with Darden's inaugural, my work was cut out. While Jim Latimer reported on the 100-member House of Delegates, I covered the 40-member Senate. Virginia's one-party Democratic politics in the 1940s were staid and genteel, the House and Senate being governed by stately parliamentary order. But they produced a lot of news. A frock-coated sergeant at arms guarded the doorway to each chamber. The scene reminded me of 19th-century England.

Senators were almost all lawyers or businessmen. Many, like John Battle of Charlottesville, or Aubrey "Kingfish" Weaver of Front Royal, were eloquent speakers. Others, like huge Harry Stuart of Elk Garden, were wits and practical jokers. There were no female or black legislators then.

I was shocked one day when Senator Lloyd Robinette of Lee County arose in the Senate, wearing a starched collar and boutonniere, to complain about Easter Week shenanigans at the University of Virginia—a recurrent complaint. Senator Robinette had been halted while driving near the University lawn early one morning, en route to Richmond, by a gang of young men in evening clothes, playing touch football in the road.

One of the students had leaned into the Senator's car, Robinette said, and said, "Sir, this is a *shit* inspection station. Do you have any *shit* on board?" The Senator, who was known in the Assembly for his formality, shook his wattles in dismay as he described it to the Senate.

The Senate heard him soberly but took no action. Boys will be boys.

That Friday, I drove Lieutenant Governor Saxon Holt and Delegate George B. Collings home to Newport News for the weekend, driving Mr. Holt's car. At Diascund Creek on Route 60 near Williamsburg, Mr. Holt asked me to stop and fetch creek water in paper cups so we could all have a drink. I half filled each cup, avoiding tadpoles and bull gudgeons, and our host poured bourbon for us from a bottle of Old Guckenheimer in his glove compartment.

"There's nothing like bourbon and creek water," the Lieutenant Governor said. Major Collings and I agreed warmly, taking it on faith.

The Peck's Bad Boy of the Senate then was Aubrey Weaver of Front Royal, who had big, frog-like eyes and a broad slit of a mouth. He was the Senate's human adding-machine, digesting budget figures instantly and spitting out totals like a cash register. He was a top lawyer and represented in her first divorce Wallis Warfield, later the Duchess of Windsor. I was saddened when he died years later in a fire at the Hotel Jefferson.

In those days, before Republicans became numerous in Virginia, legislators met peaceably in morning committee sessions in the Capitol, then convened for separate House and Senate sessions at noon, and finally adjourned in the afternoon for drinks in their rooms before supper or at the Occidental, Rueger's, Ewart's Cafeteria, or the Commonwealth Club. Legislators' pay was modest, so most law-makers roomed modestly at the John Marshall, Richmond, Murphy, or Rueger

Hotels. They usually grabbed a stand up lunch at Chicken's snack bar in the basement of the Capitol. A sign over Chicken's counter read, "Hard-boiled Eggs, 10¢/Rooster tax, 5¢."

Virginia Historical Society

Miller & Rhoads, which faced Broad Street, was at its height as a luxurious department store during World War II. Its Christmas windows and decorations were famous.

Law-makers' wives loved to come to Richmond and stay for the whole session, for Miller and Rhoads and Thalhimers' were luxurious department stores, and the Mosque and Lyric Theatre offered night entertainment. A ladies' lunch was a treat at Miller and Rhoads' tearoom, with bald Eddie Weaver of Loew's playing hit tunes on the organ, and fashion models sashaying between tables to show off the latest styles. One of them, Willis Lathrop, now Mrs. Bayard Starbuck, took pride in the fact that she had been called "the best-dressed poor girl in Richmond." She explained that her mother had made her stand up straight, buy cheap clothes from Lerner's (one size too big because "cheap clothes are cut small"), and *always* change the buttons. She remains in demand to this day as a model.

Like other old cities, Richmond had creature comforts I'd never known in Johnny-Come-Lately Newport News. On Grace Street, Montaldo's fashion shop trotted out cocktails to appease husbands while their wives tried on dresses. The Hotel Jefferson kept live alligators in a pool in its lobby, a few feet from Valentine's statue of Jefferson. There were good things to eat everywhere, and the City Market sometimes had terrapins. In fall there were chinquapins, scuppernong grapes, and damsons for jelly.

Restaurants offered little variety except for the Capri and a few other Italian spots, but Richmond was big on Southern soul food. (I was fascinated by the name of Belcher's Cafe, but never tried it.) Ewart's Cafeteria on Fourth Street was popular with us newspaper people for its turnip salad cooked with "side meat," its batter bread, sweet potatoes, cabbage with ham hock, and fried chicken glopped up with what Dick Carter (Mr. Cottrell's successor as state editor) called "all-purpose gravy." It went equally well with beef, pork, or poultry.

One familiar business I found in Richmond was the E. M. Todd Company, meat packers. From my Smithfield beginnings I knew it was a meat export firm begun by one Mallory Todd, of Bermuda, in tiny Smithfield in the 1840s. The Todd company operated for most of its life in Smithfield on the Pagan River wharf side (Mallory Todd's townhouse survives), until the company was bought and moved to Hermitage Road and Leigh Streets in Richmond.

Richmond parties were home affairs except for brides' and debutantes' receptions, and caterers were used. Cole's on

Virginia Historical Society (Foster Collection)

Loew's State was Virginians' favorite theatre, with Moorish decor under a ceiling of twinkling stars. It boasted, "All the big ones come to Loew's."

Franklin Street, next to the Woman's Club, would supply ice-cream frozen in the form and color of fruit, guaranteed to slide off your plate in the middle of the party and land on the floor beyond reach. Another Cole's specialty was the Madame Eva, a chocolate caramel with toasted almond inside, anathema to tooth fillings.

At the Woman's Exchange ("Do you *really* exchange women here?") on Franklin Street, you bought homemade mayonnaise and a cheese concoction called Lulu Paste. And at Sarah Lee's —a food shop which later changed its name to Sally Belle's Kitchen when a national chain chose the name "Sarah Lee"— you could buy luscious cakes and presents for house parties.

Richmond attracted hordes of widows as residents, many moving from rural Virginia for companionship after a husband's death, to an apartment or row house. The Fan District was full of widows and newlyweds. To accommodate these were downtown dining rooms that served monthly meal subscribers like old-fashioned boarding houses. I remember Mrs. Milton's, Mrs. Morton's, the Gresham Court, and the Chesterfield Apartments dining room.

In that era of simple food no eating place was more popular than White's Tea Room, which for years served sweets and ice cream on Grace near Loew's and Miller and Rhoads. It later branched to Cary Street near the Byrd Theater. Out-of-towners drove to Richmond just to enjoy White's hot fudge sundaes and its ice cream. But an equal attraction to me was its genteel waitresses, who looked to be the Colonial Dames of black Richmond.

Night life was limited in wartime Richmond, which was understandable in a church-oriented WASP town in the South. Dr. Freeman explained editorially that Richmond's social life centered around its homes and churches. You seldom went out to a party or dinner except on Saturday night and then you'd go to the Country Club of Virginia, if you belonged; it was *the* Country Club, though others existed for "new money." Other night spots were the Westwood Supper Club, Tantilla Gardens,

Virginia Historical Society

Franklin Street in World War II remained an area of fine homes. At left, between Second Baptist Church and Jefferson Hotel, is Archer Anderson mansion, later torn down.

and the Marshall Room at the Hotel John Marshall, but they closed early. It was against the law to dance on Sunday.

I could easily understand the gripes of the service man who poured out his complaints to Agnes Moyler Jones.

After one of his daily press briefings in the Capitol, Governor Darden asked me to stay behind and talk to him. He told me with mischievous pleasure that he planned to shake up fraternity life at State-supported colleges and would announce it next week. Although an alumnus–and later to be president–of the University of Virginia, he was disturbed by incidents there like that reported by Senator Robinette. He wanted more high school boys to go there instead of so many preppies. "Why, the University of Virginia is even more bourbon than Princeton," he thundered. "Only prep school graduates can get into a lot of fraternities there."

When I reported this to Mr. McDermott, the paper sent me surreptitiously to Charlottesville to observe student life in the then all-male school. My first stop was the Phi Gamma Delta house, to which Darden had belonged as an undergraduate. I found that, as he had said, only a few top social fraternities, largely made up of men from private prep schools, had a voice in selecting classmates for some undergraduate honors. It was indeed a preppies' world.

When Darden's reforms were announced, they created a violent reaction at the University and among its alumni. Not all were implemented, but when he became president of his alma mater after his governorship, Darden changed the school dramatically. Under his leadership it advanced academically and began to admit both blacks and women, changing forever its "bourbon" character.

Though Colgate Darden was limited as governor by wartime emergencies, he was a great success. In time, even the "bourbon" University of Virginia conceded the wisdom of most of his changes there.

Author's Collection

Old James River canal locks have been preserved by Reynolds Metals and other Richmonders, recalling days when "upcountry" produce reached Richmond by barge. The canal ceased in the Civil War.

4

V. Dabney Versus Segregation

AMERICA IN THE 1940s was deeply divided over the treatment of blacks, who made up over a fourth of Richmond's population. For years they had been relegated to "the wrong side" of Broad Street, where they ran their own community. Why was their political status not equal to whites'? Fortunately, the Bryan newspapers and especially editor Virginius Dabney in the *Times-Dispatch* campaigned for fairer treatment of blacks. That fact had attracted me to work for the paper in the first place.

Blacks in the South then had to ride at the rear of buses and streetcars and were denied admittance to many stores, hotels, restaurants, and theaters south of Broad Street in "white" Richmond. Why did they have to be second-class citizens?

The issue was not confronted until the Supreme Court in

Newport News *Daily Press*

Senator Harry Byrd caresses his spaniel, Spam, in his Washington office. Byrd controlled Virginia's conservative Democrats for 40 years.

1954 issued its world-shaking decision, styled Brown v. Board of Education of Topeka, Kansas. But the matter was being hotly debated in the press in the 1940s, and it continues to be.

Fortunately, many of Virginia's best lawyers, jurists, educators, and journalists were trying to move public opinion in the right direction, though the Byrd machine stood pat.

~ ~ ~

Virginius Dabney, editor of the *Times-Dispatch*, was the tall, quiet, soft-spoken son of historian Richard Heath Dabney of the University of Virginia. He was a Southerner in the best sense, though he was no tub-thumper. Like many Americans, he saw that the nation could not go on treating blacks as inferiors, forced to defer to whites. His *Times-Dispatch* editorials were trying to change that.

People called the paper communist or radical, but that didn't turn it from its course. Recognizing Dabney's contribution, the Pulitzer committee in the 1940s honored him with its prize for editorials. Supporting the paper's policies were Fred Seibel's political cartoons, some of the nation's best. They helped people see the wrong of racism and the need for change.

Daily the *Times-Dispatch*—and to a lesser extent the *News Leader*—tried to influence the Byrd organization to change the laws to meet Virginia's racial and social needs, but it was slow going.

~ ~ ~

In my rounds to gather news, I seldom saw Harry Byrd, Senior's network in action, but it was there behind the scenes. The Senator had been a progressive young governor from 1926 to 1930, inheriting the political skills of his father, Richard Evelyn Byrd, and of his uncle, Henry Flood. Both had been follow-

Author's Collection

Richard Evelyn Byrd, II, brother of Senator Harry Byrd, inspired Americans in the 1940s with his expeditions to Antarctica.

ers of Senator Thomas Staples Martin of Charlottesville, who had taken over the Democratic machine leadership from earlier agrarians, going back beyond the Civil War.

Most Virginians, like me, had admired Byrd as a can-do governor, but many of us found it harder to accept his later leadership as a "machine" or organization boss after he went from the state capital to Washington as a senator in 1933.

The strength of the Byrd machine lay in Virginia's optional poll tax of $1.50 per person per year, which reduced the number of Virginia's voters, most of them being white, conservative, and with middle or upper incomes. These Democrats ardently supported Byrd's pay-as-you-go policy, which he argued precluded a recurrence of the debt that had shackled Virginia after the Civil War.

On balance, Senator Byrd was an honorable man who believed in keeping government austere, abstemious, and honest. (Byrd once wrote the director of admissions at the University of Virginia that he would be expected as senator to recommend potential students but that the University should use its own judgment in admitting them.) But in racial matters he was less reasonable.

Byrd in the 1940s lived among his orchards at Berryville between senate sessions in Washington. He was seldom in Richmond, but he handpicked all but one of the governors who succeeded him until the 1970s. He enforced loyalty on appointees through the State Compensation Board, headed by Senate Clerk Everett Randolph Combs, which set state officials' salaries. If you strayed from Byrd's program, you could say goodbye to any salary raises.

Senator Byrd was not given to jocularity, but he relished two stories about the Richmond visit of Winston Churchill when Byrd was governor and Churchill came to Richmond visiting the battlefields of the Civil War. The Byrds invited Churchill to stay at the Governor's Mansion, and Churchill accepted.

On Churchill's first night, the Byrds entertained him at a black-tie dinner at the Governor's Mansion. R. Gray Williams, a Winchester attorney, was also a house guest of the Byrds and was in the drawing room when Churchill came downstairs before dinner. Mistaking Williams for the butler, Churchill asked him for a cigar. "I don't have one, sir," Williams replied, "but I'll get you one." He hot-footed it across Capitol Square to Scher's Confectionery and returned with several splendid stogies. He wouldn't accept Churchill's tip.

When Churchill asked for brandy, evidently unaware that Virginia was legally dry, Byrd put in an emergency call to his friend John Stewart Bryan for the loan of a bottle. In those Prohibition times brandy was rare, but Bryan rushed a bottle to the governor. Churchill consumed so much that Byrd had to open another bottle the next night.

As the Byrds bade Churchill goodbye at the end of his visit, Mrs. Byrd turned to her husband. "Harry," she said, "I don't know much about Mr. Churchill, but I hope you won't invite him to this house again."

Author's Collection

Author's Collection

Times-Dispatch *cartoonist Fred Seibel's drawings were picked up by many papers. This* Times-Dispatch *1943 cartoon depicted independent Democrat Francis Pickens Miller's assault on the conservative Byrd machine. Byrd candidates usually won, aided by the "organization."*

State offices were relatively few when I covered Capital Hill, for economy was Byrd's watchword. Still, jobs could be found for widows of the party faithful. For example, Virginia had a three man board of movie censors to screen Hollywood's products, even though the Hays office watched over the moral content of Hollywood's films. When I met the three grandmotherly ladies who made up the state censorship board, I realized why movies in Virginia had so many cuts.

Everybody in Richmond also joked about the advanced age and girth of Virginia's adjutant general, S. Gardner Waller, who was supposed to train our national guardsmen for the war. But nobody had misgivings about the fitness of General James A. "Olie" Anderson, who ran the Highway Department. He'd been a classmate of my father's in the VMI class of 1913, and later commandant of cadets. He talked so loud you could hear him through his office walls.

I encountered Governor Darden and General Anderson one Saturday when I attended the wedding of my cousin, Gus Edwards, of Smithfield, to Nancy Brown at St. James' Church on Franklin Street. With the war breathing down our necks, many of my contemporaries were getting married. I begged off work early that afternoon for the wedding, absentmindedly carrying my newspaper as I was escorted up the aisle. At the reception I met a bright-eyed brunette who had gone to school at St. Catherine's with the bride. Her name was Betsy Gayle, and I would think of her often when I went off in the Navy. After the war I married her and we've lived happily ever after. But that's another story.

That Christmas the paper sent me to Capitol Square to report on the annual civic pageant on the Capitol portico. A stout local thespian named Rose Kauffman Banks directed the nativity story from a remote control post, down Capitol Hill near Rueger's Hotel. I sat with her to get the names of actors.

Up on the portico stood the magisterial Dr. Freeman, intoning the glorious story of Jesus' birth, as he had done for Christmases past:

> And suddenly there was with the angels a multitude of the heavenly host praising God and saying
>
> Glory to God in the highest, and on earth peace, good will toward men.

But the "heavenly host" did not appear, so Rose Banks roared into her backstage microphone: "Angels! Angels! Where are those Goddamned angels?"

Suddenly the heavenly host rushed on stage, their wings fluttering, and Dr. Freeman resumed his orotund reading as if nothing had happened:

> And it came to pass, as the angels were gone away from them into heaven, the shepherds said one to another, Let us now go even unto Bethlehem, and see this thing which is come to pass, which the Lord hath made known unto us.

Every time I've heard that Christmas story since that starry night, I have thought of Dr. Freeman, solemnly proclaiming the scripture, and of dear, profane Rose Banks, sweating it out backstage. I wonder if God laughed, too.

~ ~ ~

Richmond was Waspishly ceremonial, like its British precursors, and the *Times-Dispatch* society editor helped keep it so. Mothers called her a year ahead to stake out a date for a daughter's debut or wedding. Much of the year's entertaining revolved around the dance schedule of the stuffy Richmond German. It was up to the society editor to avert conflicts in important functions. She kept Richmond's social calendar and knew which of the city's girls were "coming out" and which of the city's young men were suitable as guests.

Corbin Old, the *Times-Dispatch* society editor in my day, took these duties seriously. She had weathered many seasons and knew the egos involved. The worst problem was the young men. Many didn't answer invitations, leaving hostesses not knowing whom to expect. And young men didn't like walking in the "figures" that showed off the girls at the Christmas "coming out" ball at the Commonwealth Club.

But at least Corbin didn't put in print the thoughts she voiced in private. She wasn't like Helena Caperton, a starchy dowager who had written for a Richmond society magazine earlier in the century, when Richmond had its own city social register. In listing one debutante, Helena wrote, "Miss ________ is the first Baptist to make her debut in Richmond." The town still talked about it in my day.

~ ~ ~

Debutantes were profusely entertained at teas and cocktail parties by their parents' friends, with entertainments running from September through spring. Every debutante was expected to pay a courtesy call afterward on her party hosts, and she usually paid it on the Monday after the party. Monday was when the Woman's Club met, and hostesses would probably be at the club. All the debutante had to do was leave her card and run.

~ ~ ~

When February came, Richmonders burrowed in until Easter, giving up drinking, dancing, card-playing, and other innocent pleasures. They called it Lent and explained it was a time-honored observance of God's will. It meant you went to church every Sunday and gave up whatever small pleasures delighted you otherwise, theorizing that whatever was pleasurable must be sinful. Richmonders even had a joke about it:

> Mae West to a good-looking young man: "You're some kinda dream boat, fella. Why don'cha come up and see me sometime?"
>
> Gent: "I can't, Mae. It's Lent."
>
> Mae West: "Well, when you get it back, come up and see me sometime."

On Easter Sunday pious Richmonders joyously celebrated the end of Lent, often with an after-church party to end those forty dolorous days. When I walked to work down Franklin Street on Easter Sunday afternoon, I heard the tinkle of glasses and laughter. Easter was a big occasion in Richmond—especially if you'd observed Lent.

I learned that the biggest Easter parties were those of Colonel Henry W. Anderson, a bachelor partner in the firm of Hunton Williams Anderson Gay and Moore (now, thankfully, just Hunton and Williams) and of Mr. and Mrs. John Bocock, all staunch Episcopalians. They occupied adjoining mansions on Franklin Street, both now part of Virginia Commonwealth University.

Valentine Museum

Lincoln biographer Carl Sandburg paid a visit to biographer Douglas Freeman when Sandburg came to lecture in World War II Richmond.

One night I was dispatched to cover a teachers' dinner to be addressed by Carl Sandburg, who had come up from his home at Blowing Rock, North Carolina. The rest of us were in evening clothes, but the earthy poet wore a turtle-neck sweater his wife had woven from the wool of goats she milked daily at their mountaintop home, now a Park Service museum.

Sandburg spoke eloquently, but at one point he expressed regret that Virginia had forsworn Jeffersonian principles to permit one politician—Senator Harry Byrd—to exercise political decisions that Sandburg thought should be made by the people.

One dinner guest that night was Violet McDougall Pollard, widow of John Garland Pollard, who in 1930 had succeeded Harry Byrd as governor. When Sandburg criticized Byrd, Mrs. Pollard rose and stopped him dead in his tracks. She informed him politely that Virginia not only approved but warmly appreciated Byrd and his policies.

Sandburg heard the lady out and then contrasted the merits of popular democracy with the shortcomings of a political machine. I was proud of Mrs. Pollard's courage, but in principle I had to agree with the poet.

Byrd lived at Berryville, in the uplands of northern Virginia. He loved to bike up "Old Rag," a nearby mountain, and scan the lovely countryside. All Democratic aspirants for the governorship of Virginia and most other high offices trooped up to Berryville before announcing to seek the senator's blessing. In that one-party era, only Byrd Democrats were apt to win.

Richmond Newspapers

Harry Byrd often hiked up old Rag mountain near his home in Berryville. He is followed by his spaniel, Spam, one of a succession of his "office dogs."

Racial problems were growing, even in gentle old Richmond. Occasional rumors of black unrest were heard, stirred by lynchings and segregation protests from the Deep South. One night I heard that Eudora Ramsey Richardson, who had edited the Virginia Guidebook in the WPA series, was organizing Richmond blacks to seek higher domestic pay. Most Virginia households then paid only a dollar or two a day, plus carfare, with Thursday and Sunday afternoons off. The rumor seemed plausible, for Mrs. Richardson was a political activist from the Deep South.

"My goodness, where did you hear that?," Eudora demanded when I phoned her. She said she had heard the rumor but denied it. Even so, the war and the New Deal's Fair Labor Standards Act of 1938 were forcing employers to raise servants' wages. Some blacks were moving north in search of higher pay. Soon domestic help would become unaffordable to most households. Even so, skilled blacks continued to hold on to domestic jobs, like the popular "sewing ladies," Minnie and Patience, of Jackson Ward, who hired out at so much per day to come to your house to darn socks and make women's and children's clothes. Similarly, the "hair lady," Dahlia Martin, came to patrons on schedule to give shampoos.

Alas, the motherly and obliging cooks and "sewing ladies" Richmond had loved for generations would soon become a thing of the past. A lot of Richmonders blamed Eleanor Roosevelt.

5

Byrds, Bees, and FFVs

AS I TYPED AWAY one afternoon in the newspaper's city room, I felt a hand on my shoulder. It was John Stewart Bryan, the publisher, a tall, elderly gentleman with high forehead and rimless glasses. When I stood up, he congratulated me on a news story I had written. A convivial man, he often strolled through his newspapers to meet new employees and greet old ones. Some reporters were embarrassed, but I wasn't.

From then until I left Richmond for the Navy, I saw Mr. Bryan rarely, but I liked what I knew. He hired good journalists to run his papers and gave them a measure of independence. He was a versatile man who had gone to the University of Virginia and to Harvard, and his viewpoint was broader than most Virginians'. He was president of the College of William and Mary when I first knew him, turning over most of

Author's Collection

John Stewart Bryan, as president of William and Mary, entertained at the annual college yule log party. Here he welcomes Abby Aldrich Rockefeller in costume.

his newspaper interests meanwhile to his hired publisher, John Dana Wise, and later to his son Tennant.

The two Bryans were very different: the elder an old fashioned moderate and the son a conservative. But they were alike in their tall physique, whimsical humor, and their paternal attitude toward employees.

I first saw John Stewart Bryan at Fancy Dress at Washington and Lee when I was a student. President Francis Gaines had invited him with Mrs. Alfred I. duPont, a wealthy benefactor of Southern colleges. Clearly, Dr. Gaines and Mr. Bryan were rivals for Mrs. duPont's largesse. As the long night wore on, Mrs. duPont and Mr. Bryan resorted to playing patty-cake in the chaperons' box. Exclaimed one W&L professor, "Look! Mr. Bryan's patty-caking Mrs. duPont right out of all her money!"

Mr. Bryan headed William and Mary for over a decade until 1942. The college greatly improved in his tenure, helped also by John D. Rockefeller, Jr.'s revival of Williamsburg, which also encouraged the state to support the once-forlorn college more generously.

Because his wife was under treatment in a Richmond sanatorium, Mr. Bryan lived at his home, Laburnum, in Richmond, and commuted weekly to Williamsburg, driving his Franklin over Route 60 through Bottom's Bridge, Providence Forge, and Toano to Williamsburg. Sometimes as he drove he dictated to his secretary, Miss Cora Tomlinson. He turned over responsibility for day-to-day college operations in Williamsburg to Bursar Charles E. Duke, Jr., whose wife, Virginia, entertained for Mr. Bryan at the President's House.

To faculty and students, Mr. Bryan used the same hands-on-shoulders salutation he gave his news staff, greeting most as "dear girl" or "dear boy." In that depression and wartime era, when the college was struggling, his college parties delighted the hard-up students. He paid for most out of his own pocket.

One day Mr. Bryan asked Mr. Rockefeller what college president might best give Bryan tips on how to do his college job. Rockefeller suggested Dr. Ernest Hopkins, who headed Dartmouth, where Nelson Rockefeller had just gone. Mr. Bryan wrote Dr. Hopkins for advice, but the educator deprecated his own skill. "If I have any success with my boys," he wrote, "it's because I sit in the bleachers with them at ball games and eat peanuts."

To advise Mr. Bryan, Hopkins sent Dartmouth's Dean E. Gordon Bill to Williamsburg to talk with him, and they became friends on repeated visits. Thanks to Dartmouth, William and Mary took an Ivy League turn and raised its standards. Bryan also had the Harvard Board of Overseers, of which he was a member, meet at the college, and he and young art professor Leslie Cheek, Jr., continued to stage extravagant revels at Christmas and graduation.

The Christmas production began with a yule log ceremony with faculty and guests in costumes as nobles. Dr. and Mrs. Douglas Freeman were Lord and Lady Westbourne, the name of their house in Westhampton. Bryan, in full wig and waistcoat, was Lord of the Revels. After fraternities and sororities had presented their skits, His Lordship invited guests to the buffet and punch bowls, mildly spiked. Many of the "nobles" looked vaguely self-conscious, but not Mr. Bryan. He loved parties and dressing up.

When Dean Grace Warren Landrum objected to one coed's scanty costume, Professor Cheek explained, "She's Greek." Responded Dean Landrum, "She's too Greek for me!"

A memorable sight one Christmas was of the tall, angular Bryan swinging his partner, Abby Aldrich Rockefeller, around in the Virginia reel. Her quiet husband, John D., Junior, did not participate. Some Williamsburgers called the Rockefeller and Bryan years "William and Mary's golden age."

On the *Times-Dispatch* bulletin board one night appeared three photographs from a new Richmond Newspapers pamphlet, showing John Stewart Bryan, Tennant Bryan, and Dr. Freeman. When no one was looking, I lettered John Stewart "Father," Tennant "Son," and Dr. Freeman "Holy Ghost." Nobody knew who was guilty of such cheek, and I certainly didn't tell them. They can't fire me now.

Edith Lindeman was the *Times-Dispatch* amusements editor. She had married Woolner Calisch, son of Rabbi Calisch of Richmond's Temple Beth Ahabah. A bright, attractive extrovert, she got to know the Hollywood stars on her annual trips to California to write about coming movies.

When Edith's and Woolner's 25th wedding anniversary neared, actors of Barksdale Dinner Theatre in Hanover Courthouse surprised them at a party with a "This Is Your Life" theme. Unbeknownst to Edith, they brought to town her past teachers, kinsmen, and far flung friends. Reenacting her Richmond wedding, all survivors of the wedding party surprised her by appearing onstage dressed as they had been on the wedding day. Ruth Thalhimer, wife of realtor Morton Thalhimer, fitted perfectly into her tiny bridesmaid's dress.

Finally, when the M.C. reminded Edith, "In the 1930s you joined the *Times-Dispatch,*" the curtain opened to reveal the entire news staff, me included. Edith, seated with family on the front row, took one look at us and burst into sobs.

A highly successful party.

~ ~ ~

Times-Dispatch wages in the 1940s were low by Northern standards and unbelievable by today's. So some of the staff formed a chapter of the Newspaper Guild to bargain with publisher John Dana Wise for higher pay. Though living costs were comparatively modest then, some of the staff had to moonlight to get by. I got a job teaching current affairs each morning, before I began my day at the paper, lecturing at Richmond Professional Institute, now Virginia Commonwealth University.

Heading RPI then was Dr. Henry Hibbs, a sensible educator who ran his school with minimal funds, inveigling cheap moonlight labor–like mine–to teach his classes. He was deaf as a post, and I had to shout to make him hear.

"Don't take any nonsense off your students," he growled at me before I started. "Adult education is the noblest conception and the poorest reality in the world." He was right, but I enjoyed it.

~ ~ ~

The Richmond papers achieved the highest level of circulation then recorded by any morning and evening sheets in

America. (The postwar decline of papers' circulation, caused by TV, had not then been felt.) The papers enjoyed high credibility, and the management wisely let each one take its character from its editorial page.

The Bryans encouraged competition between the two staffs, which were housed in separate wings of an ell-shaped building on Fourth Street. The high standing of editors Freeman and Dabney attracted many good beginners, some from Ivy League schools. Macon, Georgia, was strongly represented on the staff because Mark Etheridge, the *Dispatch*'s former publisher, had come from there. Washington and Lee also contributed in my days and later, when Charley McDowell joined the *Times-Dispatch* and Roger Mudd the company radio station.

Because the two staffs worked in separate offices, we got along well. That was in contrast to my experience in Newport News where both staffs shared one office and its typewriters. In Newport News, the guy on the other shift always left my typewriter needing a ribbon, and sometimes swiped my Nabs from the drawer. Once or twice in Newport News, angry deskmates took their quarrel into the alley and fought it out. I don't think the Bryans would have liked that.

Mo Siegel was a sad-looking little Jewish sports writer who came up from the Deep South to join the *Times-Dispatch.* He was full of witty one-liners and loved to tease. When Red McCalley revealed he'd taken me to Hortense Blair's, Mo Siegel dubbed me "The Learned Letch from Newper News." Unfortunately, it caught on with some of my lowbrow friends.

Mo was proud of being Jewish and insisted Dr. Freeman had been born a Jew named Freedman and changed his name. "Still," he used to say, judiciously, "we Jews are proud of the guy, hitting the big time here in Richmond, among

Belmont, the Gari Melchers Estate and Gallery

The celebrated Impressionist, Gari Melchers, moved to Virginia in midlife. His paintings are exhibited at his home, Belmont, run by Mary Washington College.

you lousy Episcopalians." He later became a sports celebrity in Washington.

Everybody in Richmond wanted to be a WASP, to swim in the mainstream, to belong to "the Club," "the Church," and to spend the hereafter among the well-bred corpses in Hollywood Cemetery. That's why I was pleasantly surprised when a few independent males founded the Rotunda Club in the Hotel Jefferson as an alternative to the overcrowded Commonwealth Club nearby.

(Richmonders shun diversity, and even when they travel they like to go with other Richmonders and stay in Richmond enclaves, like Virginia Beach and Delray, Florida.)

The Rotunda Club enjoyed ground-floor rooms in the Jefferson Hotel, overlooking Franklin Street. In its brief life span, it was distinguished by its remarkable men's bar, decorated by rows of fifteen beautifully done oil paintings by Gari Melchers of an exceedingly luscious–and exceedingly nude –young woman. Rumor was she had been Melchers' model when he was in Paris. We liked to think she was his mistress. In any case, he saw a lot of her, for there was a lot to see.

When Melchers died in 1932, the paintings remaining at his home, Belmont, at Falmouth, were largely divided between the Virginia Museum and the museum that remains in his house. However, neither exhibit could use those jolly nudes. That's when the Rotunda Club hit on borrowing the paintings for the Melchers bar, where such ruffians as "The POETS" (Phooey on Everything, Tomorrow's Saturday), and the "TGIFs" (Thank God It's Friday) used to sit and contemplate the human condition. Alas, both the club and Melchers' girlies have gone.

As I walked to work one day in 1942 past the Chesterfield Apartments on Franklin Street, I saw Admiral William "Bull" Halsey come out and enter a Navy car. I'd never seen Bull Halsey in person, but his photograph as a top admiral in the war against Japan was in all the papers. I knew it was Halsey.

When I reached the newspaper office, I looked up Katherine Lewis Warren, a *News Leader* reporter who lived at the Chesterfield. Yes, she admitted, Admiral Halsey had just been flown to Richmond from the Pacific in deep secrecy, to be treated by Dr. Warren Vaughan for a bad case of shingles. Dr. Vaughan was a well-known specialist, and Richmond was familiar to Halsey from his undergraduate years at the University of Virginia.

"But the editors know Halsey is in town," Lewis told me, "and that we must lay off. The Navy wants the Japanese to think Halsey is in the Pacific, ready to attack them."

So much for Admiral Halsey. And I thought I had a scoop!

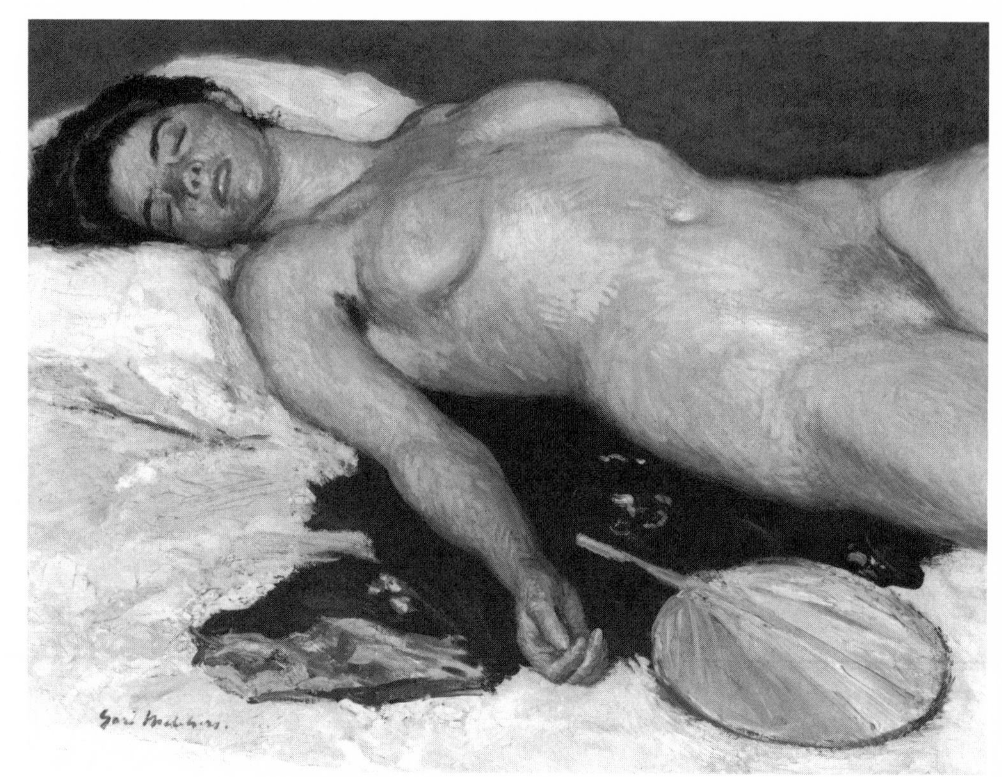

Belmont, the Gari Melchers Estate and Gallery

One of Melcher's handsome nudes is "Lassitude" now exhibited at his former estate, Belmont, at Falmouth. The same beauty posed for many of his paintings.

Proof-reading was dreadful on the papers in those days, and you never knew what misprints would show up. One society note declared that "Mr. and Mrs. Ashton Harvey were visited over the holidays by fiends from out of town." Another reported that a Richmond couple were entertaining at their home, "Bologna Arsenal." The name of the historic house was Bellona Arsenal.

Then the widow of Woodrow Wilson came to town one day

to unveil a statue of that president. Beneath a head-and-shoulders photo of Edith Bolling Galt Wilson, the *Times-Dispatch* caption began, "Unveils Bust."

Richmond's feisty Mayor Fulmer Bright had recently remarried but he stayed up all night during one year's spring rains, when high water in the James threatened the Fourteenth Street Bridge. The caption under his picture read: "Spends Night on Bride."

Once an ill-chosen editorial filler followed an editorial lauding a deceased citizen. Unfortunately, the filler read:

> **Senator Soaper Says**
>
> The chemical contents of the human body used to be worth only 36 cents, but now the Bureau of Standards tells us they're worth a dollar. Chalk up another inflationary achievement to Roosevelt's New Deal.

The family of the deceased was not amused by the odd postscript.

One fledgling reporter before my day was said to have written a news story about damages done by woodchucks with their underground "burros." The copy desk edited the story by correcting "burros" to "burrows."

"Obviously," a copy editor told the reporter, "you don't know your ass from a hole in the ground."

Sometimes a line or two of type got out of place, with chaotic results. Overton Jones clipped an obituary which concluded:

> A grave side funeral service will be held at 4 P.M. Tuesday in the Lexington Cemetery.
>
> When you are cooking chicken, save the gizzard and heart to use in soup or gravy, or chop them and add them to an egg salad sandwich.

Another snafu resulted when these lines were placed together:

> Over their graves she erected a stone monument with the wings of the Army Air Force and bearing the inscription in English:
>
> Copyright, 1946, by the *News Leader* and *Chicago Daily News.*

Proofreading has gotten better in recent years. I'm sorry.

Back before my day, newspapers allowed a bit of levity in wedding accounts. Joe Bryan III, who worked at the *News Leader* before going north, treasured one example from that paper and revived it in his book, *Hodge Podge.*

> It was a beautiful wedding. Everything went smoothly until after the 'I Do's,' when the wedding party marched back up the aisle. The groom's grandfather had got halfway when his pants fell down. Everybody burst out laughing. He calmly bent over and pulled them up and continued walking.

Too bad newspapers don't tell you such things any more.

6

The War and Thomas Lomax Hunter

RICHMOND IN WORLD WAR II was still held by the Confederates, preoccupied with the years 1861–65, when the city had been the seat of Jefferson Davis's government. Octogenarian widows and daughters of Lee's soldiers still reminisced in the Confederate Ladies' Home on Sheppard Street, behind the Virginia Museum of Fine Arts. Equestrian statues of Confederate generals lined Monument Avenue. (Lee's had to be heightened a dozen feet when it was erected so it would stand as high as George Washington's, two miles away, even though the two were not close enough to be seen at the same time.) Confederate flags flew at football games.

But I didn't sense the full power of the Confederate past until the night I heard William Rush, the black headwaiter at the Commonwealth Club, recite Lee's farewell address to his troops. He made you feel you were on the field at Appomat-

Virginia Historical Society

The most affluent of Richmond churches is St. Paul's, on Capitol Square, whose bells ring the hours over the downtown trees. It is known for avant garde clergymen.

tox in April 1865 as the Southern hero ended the bloodshed.

Rush was a handsome, gray-thatched black man who directed the courtly black waiters serving the Commonwealth Club dining rooms. Occasionally, at a banquet for visitors, he could be prevailed on to reminisce for the guests about one evening when he drank too many "heel-taps"—half consumed highballs—and dozed off looking at Lee's portrait over the mantel. He began to dream about Lee's farewell at Appomattox.

"I saw him seated on Traveler," Rush would say to his audience, "looking out over his exhausted army for the last time. Then he began to speak," Rush said, brushing his eyes, "and I found it hard to hold back my tears."

By that time we in the audience were moved too. As a student at Washington and Lee, I had developed an attachment to Lee, which Dr. Freeman and his biography had increased. Then Rush recited Lee's words to his troops:

> After four years of arduous service, marked by unsurpassed courage and fortitude, the Army of Northern Virginia has been compelled to yield to overwhelming numbers and resources. I need not tell the survivors of so many hard-fought battles, who have remained steadfast to the last, and I have consented to this result from no distrust of them: but feeling that valor and devotion could accomplish nothing that could compensate for the loss that would have attended the continuing of the contest, I have determined to avoid the useless sacrifice of those whose past services have endeared them to their countrymen.
>
> By the terms of the agreement, officers and men can return to their homes and remain there until exchanged. You will take with you the satisfaction that proceeds from the consciousness of duty faithfully performed . . . I bid you an affectionate farewell.

I was embarrassed then to shed tears; but I could see the rest of the hearers were as moved as I was. *Life* magazine carried an article about Rush and his soliloquy.

~ ~ ~

I saw more remnants of the Confederacy when I attended my first funeral in Hollywood Cemetery. I located the cemetery's obscure entrance with some difficulty through a seamy neighborhood called Oregon Hill, but once inside I encountered unforeseen vistas of trees and valleys. Handsome Victorian memorials marked the tombs of John Tyler and James Monroe.

Often I had heard elderly Richmonders, in their cups late at night, teasing each other about "who'll be next to go south on Cherry Street" to Hollywood. A lot of them have left us in the nearly half-century since I said farewell to Richmond.

The many Confederate graves reminded me of the huge losses Lee had suffered in his defense of Richmond against General McClellan in 1862 and against General Grant in 1865. Many victims, Northern and Southern, lay in mass graves at the east end of Richmond and in adjoining Henrico County, where the bloody Seven Days' Battles were fought out in 1862. That was Richmond's saddest hour.

~ ~ ~

When author Rebecca Yancey Williams was offered a corsage for the autographing party of her book, *The Vanishing Virginian,* at Miller and Rhoads in the 1940s, she declined. "I don't like corsages," she explained to her publisher. "They mess up my dress."

"Is there anything else we could give you instead?" asked the editor from E. P. Dutton, which had published the book.

"Well, you wouldn't want to give me the thing I really need."

"What's that?"

"A load of well-rotted cow manure for my garden."

"We've never done that before," he said, after a pause, "but there's no reason we can't." Dutton sent the manure, and she loved to tell about it.

Rebecca also liked to tell of her grandmother's recollections of Robert E. Lee when the handsome old warrior visited the springs of Virginia one summer while he was president of Washington College. Becky Williams' grandmother was a young lady in those days, dancing the waltzes, quadrilles, and polkas that made up an evening's dance card at White Sulphur or Hot Springs.

Lee, who was attracted to beautiful women, was surrounded at the springs by admiring females. "He loved to be with them, my grandmother said, and to touch their lovely skin," Becky told me. "You might say he was a flirt, but I think it's the most human thing I've heard about the South's hero."

Vincent Franks, rector of St. Paul's Episcopal Church when I arrived in Richmond, called on one elderly invalid in his parish in the 1940s and was asked, "Tell me, Dr. Franks, how is the General?" When the rector asked which general, she replied, "There's only one general: General Lee."

"Oh," Dr. Franks answered. "He's dead."

"Nobody ever tells me these things," she said. "And how is Dr. Minnegerode?", referring to the Civil War rector of St. Paul's.

"Well, he's gone to his reward, too," Dr. Franks responded.

Richmonders are apt to live in the past.

Richmonders loved stories about the church, and they told many of them on St. Paul's. One was of the lay reader who

Virginia Historical Society

Author Rebecca Yancey Williams and spouse Dr. John Bell Williams frequented the Mosque for concerts when Richmond dressed up.

during one service read the lesson from the Bible mentioning ewe lambs but pronounced it "ee-wee" lambs. Another was of the addled minister who pronounced a bridal couple "joyfully loined" instead of "lawfully joined." The third was about the bride's father who unknowingly trailed his suspenders behind him as he led the bride up the aisle. These stories were told repeatedly, with names included.

~ ~ ~

I was impressed by how many Virginians used their middle names. There was not only Rebecca Yancey Williams and Emma Gray Trigg, but also John Stewart Bryan, James Branch Cabell, Edward Virginius Valentine, Douglas Southall Freeman, Thomas Nelson Page, Andrew Jackson Montague, John Garland Pollard, and Helena Lefroy Caperton. Around Virginia were more, like Francis Pendleton Gaines of Lexington, and Thomas Lomax Hunter of King George County. But the most Virginian name of all was Chiswell Dabney Langhorne Perkins, called "Chilly" by his friends.

In part, the use of middle names was a Victorian survival from years when life was more formal. But it also called attention to your bloodlines. Bloodlines are oh so important to Virginia's WASPs. As William Fitzhugh wrote in colonial times, "Better never to be born than to be illbred."

~ ~ ~

One of the old timers I met in Richmond was Thomas Lomax Hunter. He was an elderly essayist who lived near Fredericksburg and wrote a daily *Times-Dispatch* column, "As It Appears to the Cavalier." He came to Richmond every few weeks to bring his typed newspaper pieces in one pocket and pats of butter in tinfoil in another. Butter was then rationed–a war casualty–but Mr. Hunter could get it back home in King George. He couldn't abide oleomargarine.

He usually dined at the oyster bar in Rueger's Hotel, a stronghold of legislators and lawyers, where he could talk politics and the Civil War. He was strongly anti-New Deal, and his column was very popular with conservative rural Virginia newspaper readers, mostly elderly.

Tom Hunter called himself "The Cavalier" because he wrote about the inherited royalism of Virginia's onetime planter class. He thought country life instilled virtues seldom found in cities. He was convinced that Yankee commercialism was destroying the manly character bequeathed to Virginians by cavalier adherents of King Charles I, who had fled to Virginia after they lost to Oliver Cromwell in England's Civil War.

He was well aware that Thomas Jefferson argued the moral superiority of country life over city. He thought so too.

You couldn't help liking Thomas Hunter. He was witty, frank, and honest. Like H. L. Mencken, he hated pretense. He was also a loner, traveling by himself to Richmond and walking uphill to the newspaper office. He wore a wide-brimmed planter's hat, which he doffed in the fashion of Sir Walter Raleigh.

And he could talk! Sentences came rolling out like Churchill's. He was never at a loss for words. As evidence of his classical schooling, he larded his speech with Shakespeare, Aristotle, and the Bible. At the *Times-Dispatch* he paid his respects and delivered his columns first to editor Dabney. In one typical column he deplored the vanity of building big houses and living urban lives. Like John Randolph of Roanoke, he thought the ideal dwelling for a philosopher was a small farmhouse with bare floors and country cooking, where one's dogs (every gentleman has dogs) could roam at will and lick food from the owner's hand.

Deriding ostentation, he wrote:

> People who think too much about the sort of house they want are apt to let the house cheat them out of a home. A home ought to fit us like our bedroom slippers.

Virginia Historical Society

Thomas Lomax Hunter long wrote his ultra-conservative "Cavalier" column for the Times-Dispatch.

He held onto such archaic pleasures as rocking chairs, oil lamps, and family reading around a table at night. He wanted to be able to kick off his boots in the living room and to scratch his dog's head without a squawk from his wife. He concluded one column:

> I ask you, you country-born boy who has gone to Babylon [New York] and has there striven and slaved and pinched and now are a prosperous citizen, . . . is it not quite another sort of home that you are homesick for when hunting season comes? Don't you remember the homely comfort of the old farmhouse, its open fire on the hearth, the earth-intimacy of the place?

I could swallow most of the Cavalier, but I was shocked by one column he handed in, on how to cook a possum. He advised readers: "First, clean the possum thoroughly, then stuff it with well-rotted cow manure. Then cook it three hours on the fireplace coals. Then take it off, throw away the possum, and eat the cow manure."

Editor Dabney wondered whether we should print it, but he let it run. Readers expected to be shocked by Thomas Lomax Hunter.

~ ~ ~

One of the Richmonders I wrote about was a wealthy spy who had secretly served the Union there throughout the Civil War. Not all Richmonders in 1861 had favored secession, and some of them lived out the war as Unionists, unmolested in Richmond. The most notable was the spinster Elizabeth Van Lew, whose house survived till recently on Church Hill, overlooking Chimborazo Park.

I had first heard of Miss Van Lew from my classmate at Washington and Lee, Randolph Van Lew Hall, whose Yale professor father descended from Miss Van Lew's brother. Ran Hall's family owned valuable colonial Virginia manuscripts, which years later I persuaded them to give to the Library of Virginia. One was a handwritten document, signed by Governor Francis Nicholson in the 1690s, dealing with Indian problems. Had it come into Elizabeth Van Lew's hands when President Lincoln appointed her Richmond's postmistress after Grant captured the City? In that job she had the run of the Virginia Capitol, whose attic floor then held Virginia's state archives.

Lizzie Van Lew, whom Richmond author Joseph Bryan III termed "Richmond's beautiful Yankee spy," is buried in Holly-

Richmond Newspapers

Presiding Bishop of the Episcopal Church in World War II was Henry St. George Tucker. He enjoyed Virginia Beach in an inner tube.

wood Cemetery beneath a boulder from Boston's Beacon Hill. Her stone is inscribed:

She Risked Everything That Is Dear to Man
Friends–Fortune–Comfort–Health–Life Itself
All For the One Absorbing Desire of Her Heart
That Slavery Might Be Abolished
And the Union Preserved

Richmond is still trying to make up its mind about Elizabeth Van Lew.

7

Writers and Hangers-On

I WANTED TO BE A WRITER, and Richmond heightened my ambition. After all, Richmond had produced many writers—not only newspapermen but novelists like Ellen Glasgow and James Branch Cabell. The city had a literary past going back to William Byrd II, who founded Richmond in 1742 and left scandalous diaries which were just then being decoded and published.

From 1742 on, Richmond's clergy, lawyers, physicians, and journalists had dabbled in literature, giving the city a bookish flavor. John Marshall wrote a biography of Washington, William Wirt of Patrick Henry, and George Tucker of Jefferson. Edgar Allan Poe came back to Richmond to edit the *Southern Literary Messenger.* After the Civil War, Thomas Nelson Page, George Bagby and Emma Speed Sampson wrote novels of "befo' de war."

Richmond Newspapers

Author Clifford Dowdey stands before St. John's Church, where Patrick Henry spoke in the Revolution. Dowdey was a novelist as well as Civil War historian.

The Richmond I moved into also had its writers. Joseph Bryan III, nephew of John Stewart, turned out books and magazine pieces as Jay Bryan. Clifford Dowdey excelled in Confederate history and fiction. David Mays was at work on his *Edmund Pendleton, 1721–1803,* which would win a Pulitzer. And the papers had other writers like Charlie Hamilton, Rhea Talley, Isabelle Ziegler, and Sue Quinn.

My mother was a fan of Ellen Glasgow's and hoped I would meet her, but Miss Glasgow lived quietly, stone deaf and ailing, in her family home at 1 West Main Street. She was fiercely guarded by her secretary, Anne Virginia Bennett, and her Sealyham, which was unearthed from its earlier casket, and buried with her when she died. As for her friend and rival, James Branch Cabell (he dropped the "James" as time went on), I discovered that he had been widowed and was yet to remarry. He led a

Newport News *Daily Press*

James Branch Cabell was a leading American novelist in the 1940s. He and Ellen Glasgow were friends and rivals for literary honors.

reclusive life on Monument Avenue.

Richmond's clutch of authors had inspired the Modern Language Association of America to hold its 1935 national convention there, addressed by Gertrude Stein, who came from Paris, together with Alice B. Toklas, to edify the nation's English professors. Miss Stein displeased the Daughters of the Confederacy by observing that Lee's obligation in the Civil War had been to the Union rather than to Virginia; to her, he was nothing but a turncoat. The hen-shaped lady thrived on controversy.

I was fascinated by rumors of Richmond's squabbling literati. Ellen Glasgow, born in 1874, was five years older than Branch Cabell and achieved earlier and wider fame; she finally won the Pulitzer prize for her novel, *In This Our Life.* in 1942. In her old age, as she struggled with ailments, Cabell gallantly helped her with editing, revisions, and proof-reading. But when her posthumous autobiography appeared, he was angered to see that she ignored mentioning his help and instead dredged up a nasty scandal of his youth.

She wrote in her autobiography, *The Woman Within,* that in 1898 she and her sister Cary had spent a month at Williamsburg's Colonial Inn, where they learned that several students in William and Mary's Kappa Alpha fraternity might be sus-

Author's Collection

At dinner at the Cabells' house: Elliott Springs, Ellen Glasgow, Branch Cabell, his wife Margaret Freeman Cabell, and editor Burton Rascoe.

pended for suspected homosexuality. One was the well-born Richmonder James Branch Cabell, whom Miss Glasgow described as "the most brilliant youth in the student body."

Ellen Glasgow went on to tell how "the leading middle-aged intellectual of the village . . . had exercised pernicious influence over some of the students, and the faculty of the College . . . had banished him forever from Williamsburg." They planned to dismiss Cabell and other participants, but Cabell's mother got the verdict reversed.

Though exonerated and eventually graduated, young Cabell was deeply embarrassed. He never referred to the incident, and never took interest in the college.

From the grave, Ellen Glasgow came back to titillate Richmond with this story and to injure an old friend. Still, it made good reading. She also denigrated her erstwhile inamorata, Colonel Henry W. Anderson, who had apparently abandoned her as lover during his World War I Red Cross service in Europe for the more flamboyant Queen Marie of Rumania. Richmonders relished gossip about this odd triangle.

~ ~ ~

When I received an invitation to join the Virginia Writers' Club, I thought I was halfway to fame. Here was my chance to meet writers—maybe even Ellen Glasgow and her ear trumpet. The first meeting I attended was at Paxton, the West End mansion of Mrs. Richard Reynolds, Sr., whose husband had founded Reynolds Metals Company, which had moved to Richmond. Mrs. Reynolds wrote poetry. Everybody would be there.

It was a black-tie affair, and I offered to drive my sponsor in a borrowed car. She was the elderly poet, Florence Dickinson Stearns, a kinswoman of Emily Dickinson. She was dressed in lace, with diamonds and a floor-length fur coat. When the butler at the Reynolds' house opened my car door to help Florence out, she threw herself into his arms.

"I feel like I'm just *burrrsssting* out of a cocoon," she exclaimed as she jumped. The butler seemed accustomed to catching ladies in midair.

When I joined her at the door, to be greeted by Mrs. Reynolds, I somehow began to doubt that Ellen Glasgow would be there, or Branch Cabell either. Most of the guests were elderly, but few had written anything I'd ever heard of. They were mostly people who wanted to write but hadn't. It was a night for genteel ladies, some smelling of mothballs from fur coats taken out of storage at Haase's fur emporium. I seemed to be the only guest under 70.

The speaker was Colonel Herbert Fitzroy, director of the Richmond Area University Center, who had been announced

Virginia Historical Society

Richmond attorney Henry W. Anderson represented American Red Cross in Rumania after World War I, where he became enamored of Queen Marie. Here they visit a Rumanian village.

as speaking on "My Night on Mata Hari," an interesting prospect. But the notice had been in error, the Colonel lamely explained when he rose to speak. His subject was actually "My Night on the Matterhorn." Shucks.

After the speech, the elderly Matthew Fontaine Maury Werth rose from his chair and invited the club to Charlottesville for its next meeting. He suggested we come "when the daffodils bloom."

"And when do the daffodils bloom?" asked a chirpy lady in the crowd.

Quick as a flash, Mr. Werth arose and rattled off lines from Shakespeare's "The Winter's Tale":

> They come before the swallow dares, and take
> The winds of March with beauty . . .

There was applause all around, and somebody shouted "Touché." Then we adjourned to the dining room.

As I drove Miss Stearns home to her apartment in the Shenandoah, I asked her "What's the biggest problem you face as a poet?"

"Writing for the mahses."

"The who?" I asked.

"The mahses, the mahses! The hoi-polloi!" she explained impatiently.

Nobody had ever used the broad "a" in Newport News, but I had to get accustomed to it in Richmond. When I grew up in Newport News, a few elderly folk stuck to such old fashioned pronunciations as "gyarden," "cyart," and even "cyarbolic acid gyargle." Such talk let you know the speaker was an old Virginia WASP, but it was hard for most non-WASPs to follow. I even got to know one lady who said she went to New York to hear "Cyarmen" and see "The Ballet Russe de Monte Cyarlo."

The two invariable WASP usages among Richmond ladies were "tomahto," as the English say it, and "receipt," which antedates the French equivalent, "recipe," now used in most households. But not in Richmond. If you're old Richmond, you say "receipt" to mean "recipe."

~ ~ ~

When novelist John Dos Passos in the 1940s moved from Europe to an 18th century farm his father had left him in Westmoreland County, the *Times-Dispatch* sent me to interview him. I phoned him, and he agreed to see me on condition that I read three of his books. I'd already read his books in Tom Riegel's critical writing course at W&L, but I reread three in case he quizzed me.

Dos Passos was recovering from an automobile accident which had killed his wife, and he and a second wife were honeymooning in his father's old brick farmhouse. We talked over lunch, and I learned that he had a bizarre background. He was the illegitimate son of a once-leading New York lawyer of Portuguese birth and of his lifelong mistress, a well-born Virginia woman.

Dos Passos the writer had grown up scarred by his eccentric parentage. A few years after I met him I was glad to see that his literary reputation was reviving. He changed from a rabid socialist to an equally rabid conservative. I caught him on the rise.

~ ~ ~

Two months before the Richmond visit of the Metropolitan Opera one spring, I was sent by the paper to New York to interview the stars who would sing in Richmond. I liked opera, and I enjoyed four days of performances with the opera manager, Edward Johnson, and Richmond's impresario, Michaux Moody, in Mr. Johnson's seats down front in the old Metropolitan Opera on 39th Street.

Between the acts, Mr. Johnson led me backstage to interview the headliners coming to Richmond: Lili Pons, Charles Kullman, Ezio Pinza, Jarmilla Novotna, Salvatore Baccaloni, and others. One night I ate steak tartare with opera stars after the performance.

Author's Collection
John Dos Passos the novelist lived in this colonial house in Westmoreland County in World War II after returning to America from Europe.

Richmond was one of a half-dozen cities then visited by the Met on its spring tour after the New York season. Local performances were in the Mosque, an Arabian Nights-style auditorium erected in the 1920s by ambitious Shriners, who had then gone bankrupt. Music lovers from all over came to the operas, which were the crowning events of Garden Week each spring.

Opera-goers then dressed up in long dresses and black tie. I saw the same ladies–and smelled the same fur pieces–I saw at the Writers Club.

The Philadelphia Orchestra also gave a series annually at the Mosque. When I interviewed conductor Eugene Ormandy, he invited me to be his

Author's Collection

Governor Tuck presented a Barter Theater ham to Helen Hayes at a Broadway show as Barter's impresario Bob Porterfield applauds.

guest at a performance with Sergei Rachmaninoff two nights later in Constitution Hall in Washington. I accepted and sat with Mrs. Ormandy and her family in the President's box while the orchestra performed a Rachmaninoff program. After intermission, the composer joined the orchestra to play one of his piano concertos.

It was an exciting evening. I shall never forget the tall, dolorous pianist shambling onto the orchestra platform in his long tailcoat. He walked pigeon-toed. In one hand he grasped a metallic hand-warmer, which Mrs. Ormandy said was to improve his hand's poor circulation. His head appeared shaved, and his huge hands stretched easily over an octave of piano keys.

It turned out to be Rachmaninoff's next to last public appearance. He died shortly afterward.

~ ~ ~

The Virginia Museum of Fine Arts, founded in the 1930s, was beginning to make itself felt as the first state art museum in the nation. One of its attractions was a biennial exhibition of Virginia paintings. A few were modernist works, criticized as "communist" by a few conventional Virginians. I thought most of them were pretty awful myself. Letters to the press derided them as efforts to undermine democracy. Wasn't Picasso a communist?

At the Monument Avenue rooming house where I lived, a mischievous commercial artist named Jimmy Swann decided to have a laugh at the museum's expense. He painted a meaningless blob of colors, typed a label to match the museum's, and hung the concoction in the exhibition when no one was looking. Jimmy's "Untitled" went undetected for days until I wrote a tongue-in-cheek exposé for the newspaper, revealing the hoax.

Jimmy became a hero in letters to the editor, but the Virginia Museum was not amused.

Bob Porterfield often came to Richmond from his Barter Theater in Abingdon, Virginia. He always stopped at the paper to see movie reviewer Edith Lindeman and promote his next play. He was a funny, stage-struck mountaineer who had founded his live theater in the midst of the Depression in southwest Virginia, accepting farm produce as barter for tickets. Sometimes he accepted live chickens. What's more, he attracted Broadway actors to perform his plays across the state.

Bob liked to twit eastern Virginians for their ignorance of the rest of the world. "From the days of the Medes and Persians," he told audiences, "the people of the coastal plain have looked down on the people of the interior as barbarians. Here in Richmond you still do." It got a laugh. It was true.

Each fall, Bob persuaded the governor of Virginia to go to New York and honor a top performer in a Broadway show with a Barter ham. The governor presented it onstage at intermission, with the press covering it to publicize Barter.

When Bob took Governor Bill Tuck to New York to give a ham to Ethel Merman in "Annie Get Your Gun," Mr. Tuck went sound asleep in the first act, seated down front in the orchestra. When Ethel wasn't belting out a song, you could hear his nasal snore all over the auditorium. Desperately, Bob shook Tuck and whispered, "Wake up, Mr. Tuck! It's time to go on!" With that, Tuck rallied and lumbered with Bob up to the stage, there to delight the audience with his Southern ham talk.

Though Porterfield was a handsome and attractive ham himself, he did not marry till late in life. In Richmond he had a coterie of admirers who trooped out to Abingdon each July and stayed at the Martha Washington Inn for Barter's repertory season—and Bob's hospitality. He was the darling of a legion of stage-struck women. I called them Bob's Barter babes.

~ ~ ~

Richmond abounded in cultural organizations, and I often wrote about them. Richmonders love to serve on boards, which Bob Munford would enumerate in his obituaries in the *News Leader.* On my reportorial rounds I often stopped in at the Virginia Historical Society, then housed in the onetime Franklin Street residence of Civil War merchant John Stewart, who had lent his house to Robert E. Lee at the end of the Civil War. The Society's director was the Reverend Clayton Torrence.

Dr. Torrence was one of the few Virginians I knew who ever spoke ill of Thomas Jefferson. He believed the statesman had been a weak and cowardly Revolutionary governor, shamefully fleeing Richmond for Charlottesville to escape the British in 1781. Worst of all, he felt, was Jefferson's youthful attempt to seduce his Albemarle neighbor, Mrs. Walker.

"It was un*think*able of Jefferson to do that," the kindly cleric would say, as if it had happened yesterday. "I shall *never* forgive him. Never."

~ ~ ~

Elderly WASPs dominated the ranks of the APVA (Association for the Preservation of Virginia Antiquities), which owned part of Jamestown island and three dozen other historic sites. My news source at the APVA was tiny, bespectacled Miss Ellen Bagby, daughter of editor and humorist George W. Bagby. She lived at the Chesterfield Apartments, a refuge for the moderately well-to-do, sometimes called "God's Waiting Room," but she spent much of her time at Jamestown, which was her lifelong passion.

As a girl Miss Ellen was plain and spinsterish, she told me, so she abandoned thought of marriage and took up John Smith and Pocahontas at Jamestown. The APVA's only guide then exhibiting the church on the island was Sam Robinson, a six-foot-three-inch black from South Carolina's Gullah country. Sam was also Jamestown's carpenter, brick mason, and grounds keeper.

Big Sam had been Miss Ellen's own discovery. One day during the Depression, when she needed help at Jamestown, she walked from the Chesterfield Apartments to "the wrong side" of Broad Street to ask a group of idle black men if one wanted a job. Sam, who'd been a circus roustabout, said "Yes, ma'am," and followed the diminutive lady to her car and his first visit to Jamestown. He proved a Godsend, for he was not only strong but anxious to learn and to inform tourists, who gave him quarter tips. They especially loved his archaic singsong and Gullah accent.

Sam had a good mind and memory. "Before long," exclaimed Miss Ellen, "he had Jamestown down pat." When the

Queen Mother of England came there, Miss Ellen instructed Sam to tell Her Royal Highness about "the mother-in-law tree" in the churchyard, which had grown up since Colonial times to separate the tombs of James Blair and his wife, Sarah Harrison Blair, whose marriage her mother had opposed. Theirs were among many faded tombstones dating from the 1600s.

Thomas L. Williams

Ellen Bagby preserved Jamestown but didn't want her heart to be buried there.

When the Queen Mother arrived, Sam bowed his head and said "Good mawnin', Madam Queen." Then he fixed his eyes above her head and went into his memorized speech:

> Now dese two [burials] in the tree there, da's one of Bob Ripley's 'Believe It Or Not." Da's Cuhnel Benjamin Harrison's oldes' daughter dere in de tree–Miz Sarah. 1687 Miz Sarah Harrison, she was in her 17. She fuhst sign a contract with a young genelman by name of William Roscow. He was 22 and she was in her 17–that she would never marry *to any man on earth* as long as he was alive, so he'p her God, signed Sarah Harrison.
>
> Three weeks later she meet Doctor James Blair, founder and commissioner [commissary] of William and Mary College.
>
> By Doctor Blair bein' a han'some ol' genelman, she breck de contract den with her lover William Roscow,

causin' his death, made of heartbreakin', an' marry to Doctor Blair when he was 39 years of age.

De parson say, 'Do you promise to love, to honor, and Obey?'

Miz Sarah say, '*No* O-bey."

Secon' time de parson say, 'O-bey?'

Miz Sarah say, '*No* O-bey.'

Thud time Miz Sarah say, '*No* O-bey,' so de parson give up an' go on wif de service . . .

The Queen Mother was delighted and told her daughter, the Queen, not to miss Sam when she came to Jamestown. She didn't.

As a girl, Ellen Bagby had been a classmate of Nancy Langhorne's at Miss Jennie Ellett's Richmond school, and Nancy occasionally came back to Virginia from England to see her old friends. When I encountered the two ladies one day, Miss Ellen introduced us, adding, "Lady Astor was the first woman to sit in the House of Commons."

"Don't be a fool, Ellen," snapped Her Ladyship, without a trace of humor. "He doesn't want to know that stuff."

Miss Ellen smiled benignly; she was used to it. She also knew Lady Astor had learned to "chaffer," as she called it, from farm hands at Mirador plantation where she grew up long ago. Lady Astor told novelist Rebecca West that she did it to establish an affectionate familiarity, to be responded to in kind.

Miss Ellen ran Jamestown as long as she could, but she never could understand why so many Americans came to see it. She resented non-Virginians. "Why do all these people flock here?" she would ask, indignantly. "Jamestown is a *Virginia* shrine!" I guess it was the WASP in her.

When she finally retired as APVA chairman at Jamestown, a testimonial speaker on Jamestown Day eulogized her and suggested that her heart should be buried at Jamestown after her death.

After the applause, Miss Ellen arose, not a bit grateful but highly indignant. "Now look-a-here," she told the speaker, who was Charles E. Duke, Jr., bursar of William and Mary. "You leave Miss Ellen's heart *alone*! Miss Ellen wants to be buried *all in one piece* in Hollywood Cemetery in *Richmond*!"

And so she was, from Grace and Holy Trinity Church in Richmond, to the strains of "For All the Saints." I was there.

8

Keeping Virginia Green

WHILE I WORKED in Richmond, the city became embroiled in a war on rats. One of my assignments was to cover a women's mass meeting at the Mosque—now the Virginia Landmark Theatre—to enlist housewives to clean up yards and spread rat poison. The poison was red squill, and the city distributed it to householders free in the town's older section, where truculent rodents ran wild at night.

A rat had bitten a child in Jackson Ward, said chairman Mrs. Robert Barton, Jr., at the Mosque meeting, and rabies might follow. The ferocious rodents had been multiplying ever since William Byrd had founded the city. It was up to the ladies to get rid of them.

From the Mosque, the ladies went forth and assailed the rats, supported by local papers and radio stations. The campaign proved a great success. The zealous ladies then went on to oppose highway billboards, and auto graveyards. "Keep Virginia Green" became the Commonwealth's rallying cry. It gave radio personalities like Irvin Abeloff, Alden Aaroe, and Fred Haseltine plenty to talk about on the air.

~ ~ ~

After Richmond debutantes progressed from prep school and college through marriage, they then confronted membership in the Junior League, the Garden Club, the Woman's Club, and finally the APVA or some historic museum. Their hardest jobs came just after Lent, when Virginia observed Historic Garden Week, run from Richmond. Garden clubs worked up to it a whole year, as seriously as Eisenhower invading Normandy. Husbands got short shrift, if any shrift at all, in Garden Week.

In her Garden Week chronicle, *Follow the Green Arrow,* Teen Martin (Mrs. James Bland Martin, late of Gloucester and president of the Garden Club of Virginia) told many incidents. But she omitted stories of the frozen bee which thawed out on one Flemish arrangement and terrorized rooms full of ladies; of a Garden Week tourist who locked herself in the Redlands plantation bathroom in Albemarle to shampoo her hair; or of a rose exhibited in a Garden Club show as "Mrs. Beverley Johnston Willis: Good in a bed but better against a brick wall." All were true stories.

~ ~ ~

Richmond in the 1940s had grown to 193,000 people, but it enjoyed some of the same informality as the little town of Smithfield where I was born. Richmond neighborhoods had distinct personalities and their own small groceries, restaurants, and drugstores. A store, a park, or a confectionery would serve as the social hub of young people. The areas I got to know—Capitol Square, the Fan, and the West End—were old enough to have a life of their own. The old downtown blocks were the quaintest with their back alleys, carriage houses, and cobblestones, which recalled 19th-century horses and wagons.

But what differentiated Richmond most from other towns was its strong church schools, which were largely single-sex schools. They created a core of privileged young people who got to know each other well in a dozen years together in class and on athletic fields, from kindergarten to college. By that time they had formed loyalties that bound them together unusually closely for life. This bothered non-Richmonders, who felt excluded.

More than most cities, Richmond is a prep school town. Boys who start kindergarten at St. Christopher's together go through its high school together, forming lifetime bonds. The same is true of St. Catherine's, Collegiate (now coeducational), St. Gertrude's, St. Benedict's, and other private schools. Children are enrolled at birth. As in New England, where private prep schools separated WASP youth from Irish immigrants, so Richmond prep schools separate old from new Richmonders.

And old Richmonders love it—most of them. In an overly permissive America, growing up as a Richmond preppie gives students a sense of belonging. (One of the few dissidents was my friend Eva Tyler Morgan Wyatt, a onetime St. Catherine's athlete. "But why did St. Catherine's keep teaching us to be *good losers*?" she asked. "Who wants to be a *good loser*?")

Brought up in small classes, Richmond's private schoolers form attachments that shape their lives. They go off to college together, marry other Richmonders, settle in Richmond, and absorb Richmond's deep-fried conservatism. Governor

Virginia Historical Society

Pratt's Castle, a 19th-century iron edifice downtown near the James, was torn down to make way for offices. Mary Wingfield Scott mourned the loss.

Darden attributed what he called the "bourbonism" of the University of Virginia in the 1940s to its prep school alumni from Richmond.

It's a way of life that satisfies upper income Richmonders, though others criticize it as elitist.

Louise Catterall was a preservationist and a prime source of information for newcomers like me. She'd gone to Miss Jennie Ellett's (later St. Catherine's) and then to Bryn Mawr, where Miss Jennie had inspired some of her best students to go. I knew Mrs. Catterall as the wife of Ralph Catterall, a Harvard law graduate and member of the State Corporation Commission. Louise's chosen work was as unpaid librarian of the Valentine Museum of Richmond history. She knew more about Richmond than anyone else in town.

Her sidekick was Mary Wingfield Scott, another product of Miss Jennie's and Bryn Mawr, who spent part of her fortune saving old Richmond. Miss Scott never got over the fact that Albemarle Paper Company tore down an unsightly antiquity called Pratt's Castle on Gamble's Hill and replaced it with a pseudo-Regency building, now the Ethyl Corporation headquarters. I heard her lament the loss.

"Those people destroyed a most historic cahstle," she declared, referring to Albemarle and squinting through her thick glasses. "It was not an ordin'ry cahstle, mind you, but a *genuine cahst-iron cahstle*! And they replaced it with a *copy* of the *Williamsburg Inn*!" She made it sound insane.

At this revelation, she paused and looked around for commiseration. Then she went on to explain that Mr. Pratt built his landmark to try out cast-iron housing. His was evidently the only iron residence ever erected. (You could see why.)

Miss Scott knew Richmond's historic houses by heart. At a City Council hearing one night on the rehabilitation of Jackson Ward, she pled with councilmen to save "prewar" houses. When one councilman asked, "Which war are you talking about, Miss Scott?" she responded, "The *Civil* War, of course," as if there were no other.

~ ~ ~

Like Miss Scott, Mrs. Catterall loved "old Richmond." She fought the changes taking place in World War II and the influx of "new people." She blamed it all on the Junior League.

"Our Richmond boys go north to college," she told me,

"and marry bright girls from the north. Then, when they move back here, the wives get involved in the Junior League. They go from there to take over the boards of our hospitals, museums, and historical societies. Next thing you know, they've taken over the whole town. I blame it all on the League."

~ ~ ~

Maria Williams Sheerin saw it differently. The daughter of attorney Lewis Catlett Williams of Richmond and wife of the outspoken Reverend Charles Sheerin, she wrote a reminiscence, *The Parson Takes a Wife*, which shook up staid Episcopalians.

She saw Richmond society as a series of concentric circles, the outer one being membership on a church vestry or of the Junior League. A narrower circle was designated "Patients in the Waiting Room of Dr. Beverley Randolph Wellford," a well-known nose and throat specialist. The inner circle was reserved for those whose choice of drinks was known to Benny Lambert, Richmond society's favorite caterer. That meant they were promptly served at a cocktail party, without even going to the bar.

~ ~ ~

Richmond never wanted to be big, and it disdained to compete with Norfolk, 100 miles away. Most "old Richmonders," like Mrs. Catterall, preferred it as it had been before World War 1. We called old Richmonders like her "Stay-Puts," as opposed to the newer "Come-Heres" and "Come-Back-Heres." Richmond had many of the latter, too, who had gone from college to make a fortune "up north" in tobacco, insurance, or some other field, and then come back to Virginia, where they'd wanted to be all along.

Richmond's revival after Reconstruction brought needed Northern capital to town. Most early tycoons dealt in tobacco, like John F. Allen and Lewis Ginter (originally Guenther), who started Allen and Ginter's cigarette factory in the 1880s to make "Richmond Gems" and help switch pipe- and cigar-smokers to the stylish new cigarettes. In the process they became multi-millionaires, along with Richmonders James Dooley, a rare Catholic, who dealt in steel and railroads, and Joseph Reid Anderson, who founded Richmond's long-successful Tredegar Iron Works.

For several generations after the Civil War, Richmond men paraded their Confederate military rank. It was a town of generals, colonels, majors, and captains. Lieutenants didn't count. But such conceits had largely died out by the time of the World Wars.

In the same era came Jewish immigrants from Europe to join earlier Christianized Jews like the Myers, Mordecais, Marxes, and Oppenhimers. Franklin Street was extended into Monument Avenue as the backbone of the city's major residential area, with equestrian statues of Confederate generals along the way to glorify it.

Those were also the years of the society belle, when society editors filled columns with tributes to the Langhornes and other beauties. Richmond's newspapers–in the early 1900s numbering five or six–chronicled the seasonal migrations of the belles.

After Nancy Langhorne married William Waldorf Astor in England in 1906, other Langhorne sisters wed titled Englishmen. Other ambitious Richmond girls also went north or

St. Catherine's School

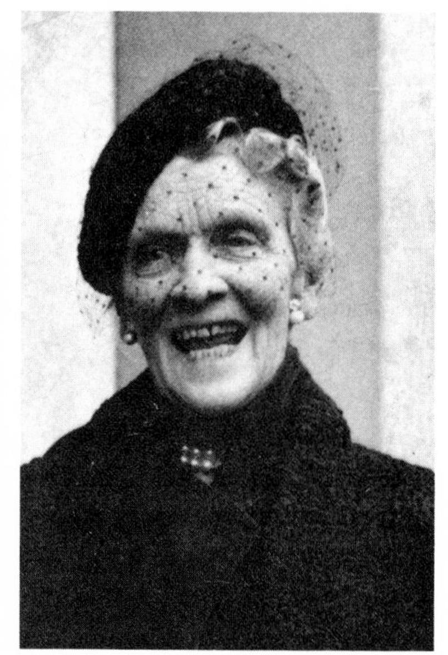

Newport News *Daily Press*

Virginia Randolph Ellett, called "Miss Jenny" by pupils, founded a school that became St. Catherine's and imposed high standards on her girls. A frequent Richmond visitor was Lady Astor, who grew up and attended Miss Ellett's school. She had many relatives there.

abroad to seek husbands, for few Richmond bridegrooms in Reconstruction years had money. Mary Triplett was one of the belles celebrated in the press, dazzling vacationers at the several dozen Virginia springs. Richmonder John B. Mordecai was killed in a duel over her in 1873 with Page McCarty, but Richmond flour magnate Philip Haxall finally walked off with her in marriage.

The witty Richmond beauty Mattie Ould defied her father, a Richmond judge, by marrying a mere Richmond editor, Oliver J. Schoolcraft. She was alienated from her family. Poor Mattie died in childbirth, unforgiven by her pa, and was buried to the strains of "Under the Daisies." And there was the romantic novelist, Amelie Rives, who married the Russian portraitist, Prince Pierre Troubetzkoy. She was also beautiful, and a Richmonder too.

Admired as these belles were by their contemporaries, their fading photographs today rarely justify their fame. But a belle by any standard was May Handy, half-sister of Mattie Ould and famed for her complexion. The Richmond *Dispatch* wrote, "She reigns as undisputed queen of love and beauty." May never braved the midday sun for fear of sunburn–pale skin was in vogue–and finally married the rich James Brown Potter of New York. Richmonders sniffed at May's accepting a divorced man, but times were changing.

Well-off Virginians continued to flock to the Virginia springs until autos and ocean bathing led to the ascension of "Virginia's Riviera" along the bay, a few years before World War 1. August was the invariable vacation month, when courts adjourned. Richmond's favorite physician, Dr. Hunter McGuire, recommended that wives and children get out of town in "dog days" of August to avoid fevers. As a result, Richmond was socially dead each summer until air conditioning resuscitated Southern summers.

After World War II, summer-long vacations at the Homestead Hotel or the Greenbrier Hotel were old hat. The automobile had put America on wheels, dooming the sedentary life of spring resorts. Only Hot Springs, Warm Springs, and a few others survive today as Virginia mountain resorts. The belles of the many other springs reign no more. You find them now at the beach or abroad.

While I was doing research at the Valentine Museum, Louise Catterall told me of a mysterious Richmond woman who had moved to New York and married Collis Huntington in the 1880s, destroying all record of her Shockoe Bottom birth. She turned out to be Arabella Yarrington, who was working in her mother's Main Street boarding house in 1869 when the big New York millionaire came to town to buy control of the Chesapeake and Ohio Railway.

Huntington fell deeply in love with the 19-year-old girl, even though he was married. After he had returned to New York and learned Belle was pregnant by him, he arranged for her and her family to move quietly to New York City, close to him. After she bore his son, Belle became a companion to Huntington's dying wife. He married her after his first wife died, building a Fifth Avenue palace for the two of them and filling it with Old Masters. Their son Archer was adopted as Archer Huntington.

After Collis Huntington died in 1900, Belle traveled the world as "America's richest widow," collecting art. In midlife she so captivated Collis's nephew, Henry E. Huntington, that he divorced his wife and married "Aunt Belle." With Belle's encouragement, he created the Huntington Library and Museum at San Marino, California. Her son Archer became a philanthropist before he died in 1955, creating the Mariners' Museum at Newport News and a dozen other museums.

Belle Huntington destroyed all record of her Richmond background to conceal her affair with Collis and to hide Archer's illegitimacy. After Belle died in 1924, Mary Wingfield Scott of Richmond made a trip to San Marino to learn more about her, but Belle had covered her tracks. Nearly all her letters had been burned, and people knew nothing but what she had told them. Only in the 1980s did a Huntington connection finally admit to Belle's Richmond background, though a few of us had known it all along.

The best place to me to observe Richmond's womanhood was the Richmond Woman's Club, the distaff equivalent of its male Commonwealth Club. It is affiliated with no other club and doesn't want to be. But each winter it has top lecturers from all over, followed by tea. For 70 years it has distributed dozens of scholarships to ambitious young Richmonders.

When I went there I was distracted when ladies in the audience began slipping out of their seats in the middle of the lecture, obscuring the slides being shown by the lecturer. "They want to be first in line at the tea-table," my hostess whispered. One silhouetted member was as short and as convoluted as a chicken gizzard. "There goes Mrs. Gizzard," somebody said. I could see what she meant.

Richmond's bland self-satisfaction rubbed non-Richmonders the wrong way. Outlanders dubbed it "the holy city." When a new member was proposed at the Woman's Club, the first question was "Who *was* she?"–not "Where does she come from?" or "Who is her husband?" And money didn't matter as much as in most cities; most of the club's ladies were content to drive Fords and Chevrolets, as the parking lot showed.

Many Richmond ladies regarded anything west of Charlottesville as uncivilized Outer Space. Mrs. Frank Gilliam of Lexington, once president of the Garden Club of Virginia, attended a Richmond lunch for a local bride and her Roanoke bridegroom. At the bridal buffet, the hostess invited Roanoke guests to "Have some cold potato soup," while urging Richmonders to "Have some vichyssoise." When Louise Gilliam's turn came, she told her hostess sweetly, "In Lexington we call it vichyssoise, too."

Author's Collection

Franklin Street was the Fifth Avenue of Richmond. There in 1906 Frederic Scott built this house, later the John Bococks'. It is now part of Virginia Commonwealth University.

Richmond's old-boy and old-girl networks were noticed even in the military. When Lieutenant General Withers Burress, onetime VMI commandant and World War II field officer, brought his wife, Ginger, to Richmond to visit his old friend, Martha Valentine Cronly, Ginger Burress observed that the girl-talk always got back to Miss Ellett's school.

Before Pinky Burress retired from the Army at New York's Governor's Island, his wife told him, "I'll retire with you anywhere but Richmond. I'm sorry, Pinky, but I just can't spend the rest of my life talking about that darned Miss Jennie."

The wife of the commanding admiral at Norfolk's Naval

Base once asked, "Why do the wives of Richmond navy officers always have to go back there to buy their clothes and have their babies?" I couldn't help her.

Of all the dowagers who graced Franklin Street, the most unconventional was Elisabeth Scott Bocock, daughter of the powerful Frederic Scott and widow of attorney John Holmes Bocock. She and her husband lived in a Franklin Street mansion next door to Colonel Henry W. Anderson.

Organic gardening was Mrs. Bocock's passion. A disciplined string-saver, like all her Scott family, she believed God meant for man to return dead animal and vegetable matter to the earth to enrich its soil, and she hounded family and friends to do the same. She prided herself on having the first compost heap in Richmond, piled up behind her Franklin Street garden.

Mrs. Bocock collected dead fish and butcher's scraps from groceries and spaded them into her compost heap, inciting one neighbor to complain of the stench. When her dog died, friends surmised that it too would end up as compost for Elisabeth's flowers.

A devotee of bicycle-riding to save wartime gas, she pedaled daily to see her dwindling circle in downtown Richmond. Deciding to get a college degree after her husband died, she enrolled at Mary Baldwin College in Staunton and took her bicycle and old-fashioned bicycling clothes with her. The college girls loved the bird-like, unpretentious lady, who gave so much pleasure to everybody! They took up a collection to buy her a gift, little knowing that "that sweet old lady" was one of Richmond's richest women.

9

Six WASP Dynasties

IN BOSTON the Cabots speak only to the Lodges. In New York, it's the Vanderbilts and the Astors. In Philadelphia, nothing can trump a Drexel but a Biddle.

And in Richmond?

Lacking any industrial giants until Reynolds Metals, A. H. Robins, and Ethyl came along after World War I, Richmond's WASPs grew up without any single towering fortune—no motor dynasties like Detroit or Robber Barons like California. Not since the death of Chief Justice John Marshall in 1835 has Richmond had one undisputed First Family.

Instead, Richmond has grown as a city of mid-sized industries, producing many families of moderate wealth. Like their WASP forebears, they have a dynastic concept: pride of place, an urge to enhance family status, and family continuity through work, investment, proper marriage, and adherence to the status quo. They are the Richmond Establishment.

Few of these wealthy dynasties go back beyond the Civil War, I learned, when Richmond was little more than state offices and a produce center. Little cash was inherited from pre-Civil War plantations, which were bankrupt after Appomattox. But Reconstruction Richmonders worked to lift their town from the ashes, and they succeeded: nearly all of Richmond's "old money" really comes from its industrialization since the Civil War. A network of families has grown rich from cigarettes, railroads, merchandising, real estate, banking, and manufacturing.

In place of the planters and merchants of John Marshall's era–Carringtons, Allans, Gambles, Mayos, Stewarts, Andersons, and the like–Richmond in the 1880s bred its first industrial millionaires. It was their luck to be born in the golden age of capitalism, before income taxes and the New Deal made it harder to get rich.

Six typical WASP survivors among Richmond dynasties are the Branches, Bryans, Reeds, Scotts, Williamses, and Valentines. Some are linked loosely by marriage, but they are similar in many WASP ways. All are Gentiles. Nearly all continue to deal in investments, banking, real estate, and the law. And though they were of mixed Protestant origins a century ago, nearly all are now Episcopalians or Presbyterians.

Most of them now live in Richmond's stylish West End, their boys attending St. Christopher's School and the University of Virginia, marrying hometown girls, and following their fathers into family firms.

As for the girls, the pattern is St. Catherine's or Collegiate, then on to "the University" or a girl's college–and maybe a

Valentine Museum

Four generations of the Branch family: John Patteson Branch, 1830–1915; John Aiken Branch, 1887–1945; Thomas Branch (the founder), 1802–1888, and John Kerr Branch, 1865–1930.

year abroad or up north to top them off. Then, after a proper wedding at St. Somebody's Church, they raise two children (preferably one of each sex) and live happily ever after. In Richmond. With frequent trips to "the Club," "the Beach," and "the Rivah."

Conventional in outlook, these families have stayed on top for five or six generations. In a quiet way, they inculcate family cohesion, marriage within the group, social and religious orthodoxy, and the need for a good bank balance. Principal–and principle–have seen them through.

Typically Anglo-Saxon, industrious, and Virginia-rooted is the Branch family, whose first English forebear reached Henrico in 1619. Seven generations later, Thomas Branch was born on his father's Chesterfield County plantation in 1802. Ambitious Tom moved to Petersburg and became a commission merchant, buying or bartering farm produce, and shipping it. In 1861 he was elected to the Virginia Convention, where he was one of a few eastern Virginians to oppose secession. However, when Lincoln called on Virginia troops to invade the South, Branch signed the secession ordinance and sent five sons into Confederate service.

After Appomattox, shrewd Thomas saw Richmond's promise, moved his family down the pike to the Capital, and founded a combined brokerage and bank on Main Street. This was Merchants Bank, one of Virginia's first, to be merged later with First, then to become part of Sovran, and finally to be part of today's huge NationsBank. Called "the father of Virginia banking," Tom Branch laid the cornerstone of the family fortune. Three other Branches–John Patteson Branch, John Kerr (pronounced "Carr") Branch, and Melville Branch, followed Thomas in the First and Merchants presidency.

After he moved to Richmond, Tom Branch placed each son in a family enterprise. John Patteson succeeded his father at Merchants and became the patriarch till he died. Like Thomas, he was active in Methodist affairs. He also gave Richmond its first public baths, whose facade fronts Monroe Park on Main Street. Their design was from Marie Antoinette's Petit Trianon.

Said a contemporary of Pat Branch, "He preached the gospel of sanitation and led the forces of progress in demanding better sewers, drainage, paving, [and] pure food." And the Branch taste for grandeur livened parochial Richmond.

Branch fortunes peaked in the generation when John Kerr Branch–John Patteson's son–ran Merchants Bank. He built a glorious Tudor mansion at 2501 Monument Avenue, designed by John Russell Pope. The family also owned Villa Marsilio Ficino at Fiesole, Italy, and a summer place at Pawling, New York. As exotic as John Kerr were his sister Margaret–who married Ellen Glasgow's brother and spent her life in England–and their brother, Blythe–who lived most of his life in Paris. Returning to Richmond rich and cultivated in old age, Blythe lived in great style that titillated the home folk. He founded the Richmond Symphony (it died in World War II, but was reborn) and was president of the embryonic Virginia Museum from 1937 till 1942.

Branch connections abound in Petersburg and Richmond. One was the eloquent Reverend Walter Russell Bowie, rector of St. Paul's Church in Richmond and then of Grace Church in New York. Another was novelist James Branch Cabell. The most beloved was Mary Cooke Branch (1887–1938), who married attorney Beverley Munford and was an early suffragist and campaigner for women and blacks. A city school bears her name.

The current Branches and their money are entrenched on

Publishers Tennant Bryan and son John Stewart Bryan III continue newspaper dynasty begun in Richmond by Tennant's grandfather, Joseph Bryan.

Richmond Times Dispatch

John Stewart Bryan published the two Richmond dailies at outbreak of World War II. He also was president of William and Mary.

Main Street. "We're investment-minded," says one. "We're also cautious, stay out of politics, and had rather work than play."

The most attractive Richmond tycoon in his day must have been Joseph Bryan (1845–1908), a Gloucester-born lawyer who moved to Richmond in 1870 after fighting for the Confederacy. He was one of Mosby's troopers and then practiced law in Fluvanna. Soon after arriving in Richmond he married Isabel Lamont Stewart of Brook Hill, daughter of John Stewart, a Scottish-born tobacco merchant. Brook Hill was the

Henrico plantation, still surviving, of the Robert Carter Williamsons, Isabel Stewart's maternal grandparents.

In an era of empire-building, Joseph Bryan stands out. Tall, handsome, and courtly, he was fiercely dedicated to Richmond's progress, along with such contemporaries as Major Lewis Ginter, Major James Dooley, and Major Fred Scott—all ex-Confederates. He merged the *Richmond Times* with the *Dispatch* and was its editor-publisher. From this and the Bryans' later *News Leader* grew today's Media General conglomerate, whose voting stock the Bryans control.

Joseph Bryan I bought—and reared his family at—Laburnum, the wealthy Lyons family's estate near Brook Hill, where his wife's Stewart mother and sisters lived. Laburnum stayed in the Bryan family till the 1940s, when grandson Tennant Bryan gave it to Richmond Memorial Hospital and moved his family to Ampthill in Westhampton. Heirs of the Stewarts still own Brook Hill, now the home of Mr. and Mrs. Peter Gates. She is the daughter of Joseph Bryan III, author and late resident of Brook Hill.

Though Joseph Bryan I never held office (he missed the House of Delegates by one vote), he was an influential figure. He and his wife were immersed in historical societies. Their sons were versatile: John Stewart, the eldest, carried on at the newspapers. Jonathan was an entrepreneur. Robert was a surgeon, St. George a dilettante, and Thomas Pinckney a lawyer. Their progeny have equally varied interests.

A close-knit tribe, the Bryans revere Joseph I, whose statue stands in Monroe Park. Son John Stewart credited his father's rise to "the habit of command," inherited from planter forebears in Virginia and Georgia. Part was also due to his skills of pen and tongue, talents passed on to John Stewart and to St. George's son Joseph Bryan III and grandson C. D. B. Bryan, both writers.

The Bryan papers were Democratic under Joseph I and John Stewart, but they became more conservative and Republican under Tennant Bryan. This continues under J. Stewart Bryan III, Tennant's son.

~ ~ ~

For a few decades before 1900, Richmond was America's cigarette capital, at a time when cigarettes were handmade. The invention of the cigarette stepped up smoking and made local tobacco millionaires: Lewis Ginter, James Thomas, Jr., Archibald and Malvern Patterson, Otway Allen, T. C. Williams, W. T. Hancock, Jacquelin Taylor, and the Arents, Whitlocks, and others. But James Buchanan Duke's rival American Tobacco Company in New York eventually bought the rights to the automatic cigarette-making machine, which made cigarettes cheaper, and industry dominance passed out of town to Duke.

Even so, Richmond remains a tobacco center. There the local firm of Larus and Brothers, a prosperous one, flourished from Reconstruction until 1968, when it was bought by Rothmann's of London. To Larus' presidency in 1908 came William T. Reed, Sr., (1864–1935), who was a protégé of his mother's brother, Charles Larus. Reed was the second oldest of seven remarkable brothers reared on Church Hill, all of whom made fortunes.

The first of these Reeds in Virginia was Elias, who came from Massachusetts to City Point (Hopewell) in 1807. His son William Block Reed moved to Richmond before the Civil War and died young, leaving widow Mollie Larus Reed to rear a big family. Under her brother Charles' influence, five of Mollie's sons went into tobacco. The Larus company invested early in radio and television, operating WRVA radio and TV until it sold them in 1968.

Two Reed brothers, Leslie and Wellford, rose to be direc-

Virginia Historical Society

Prominent in prewar Richmond were Mr. and Mrs. William T. Reed, Sr. He was one of the Reed tobacco dynasty and a mainstay of the Byrd organization. He was a lifelong Democrat.

tors of huge Imperial Tobacco Company of Great Britain, each in turn running American operations from Richmond. A sixth Reed, Stanley, created Manchester Board and Paper, and a seventh, Charles C., co-founded Williams and Reed wholesale dry goods. The Reeds were go-getters.

But the Reed family keeps a low profile and claims to be "as plain as an old shoe." The most visible was William T. Reed, Sr., a power in the Byrd machine, who died in 1935. "We don't want Virginia to change," he declared when Harry Byrd became governor in 1926. Reed was "like a father" to Byrd.

Reeds are Presbyterians, go to Hampden-Sydney, and like the outdoors. Among their fine houses is beautiful Sabot Hill in Goochland, which Mr. and Mrs. William T. Reed, Jr.–she was Mary Ross Scott–restored. Indeed, the Reed-Scott union in the 1930s was notable in Richmond as a merger of dynasties–she representing Scotts and Branches and he Laruses, Lathrops, and Reeds. It was a far cry from those families' Reconstruction beginnings in Petersburg and City Point.

Of all Richmond dynasties, I found the Scotts the most lordly. What other has a 3,913-acre Blue Ridge enclave with cottages for kin and friends? Or has given a stadium to the University of Virginia? Or has a summer home designed by John Russell Pope?

"We have very very firm opinions on all subjects," wrote the late Fred W. "Freddie" Scott III, of Albemarle, grandson of the immigrant Scotch-Irish youth who came to Petersburg from County Donegal in the 1850s and generated the Scott clan in Richmond. It was he–Frederic Robert Scott–who married Sarah Frances Branch, daughter of Petersburg tycoon Thomas Branch, in 1857 and who moved down the pike to Richmond after the Civil War. Ensconced in big houses on

Franklin Street, Scotts and Branches pooled money to build Richmond into the financial and industrial center it is today. Banks, brokerages, and railroads resulted.

Frederic Robert Scott and his wife had nine children. Known as Major Scott or Fred Scott, he ran the Richmond and

Virginia Historical Society

Mrs. Frederic W. Scott in 1904 entertains three of her five children. Her husband started Scott and Stringfellow and built a Franklin Street mansion.

Petersburg Railway (later Atlantic Coast Line) in Reconstruction and was a power in his father-in-law's Merchants Bank.

After "the Major" died in 1898, the presiding Scott was Frederic W., who founded Scott and Stringfellow brokerage in 1893, and made millions in railroad reorganizations. Thanks to his lordly style, he dominates family lore, which is kept alive by family summerings at his onetime Royal Orchard estate in Albemarle County's mountains. (It had grown Albemarle pippins for Queen Victoria and thus got its name.) Scott bought the land in 1902 and had architect Pope design the house. It is now enjoyed by descendants, who share it as a family country home.

Women of the Scott clan share the firm opinions the Scotts are known for. As their inspiration, they point to great-grandmother Sarah Frances Branch, who married "the Major." They also remember the bluntness of maiden Aunt Frances Branch Scott–"Aunt Boxie" (for "chatterbox")–an early suffragist. She was a favorite of such uninhibited nieces as Mary Wingfield Scott, Elisabeth Scott Bocock, Isabel Scott Anderson, and Mary Ross Scott Reed, called "Rossie."

Says a Scott in-law, "A Scott can always tell you how to run your business." Within the family, nobody seems to mind.

Though Richmond's prominent Williamses are often taken to be one family, they're actually three or four. The current Richmond phone book has 24 columns of Williamses, a profusion that led one churl to write:

> Here's to Confederate Richmond,
> Defended by General Lee's sword,
> Where the Williamses flourish like bay trees
> And the Bryans converse with the Lord.

Virginia Historical Society

Progenitor of many current Richmonders was John Langbourne Williams, 19th-century businessman and grandfather of 56 children of the "Railroad" and "Pious" Williams clans.

Perhaps the best-known Williamses are the "Railroad" Williamses, as descendants of John Langbourne Williams (1831–1915) and Maria Skelton Williams are sometimes known. They had 56 grandchildren. The family included four conspicuous sons: Seaboard Railway founder John Skelton Williams; attorney Edmund Randolph Williams of Hunton, Williams; Postmaster Berkley Williams of his father's firm, John L. Williams and Sons; and Dr. Ennion G. Williams, first health commissioner of Virginia, who was a pioneer in radiology.

That much is simple, but the rest of the Williams story is complicated. To confuse matters, John Langbourne Williams's daughter, Maria, married attorney Lewis Catlett Williams (no kin), of Orange County, thus giving rise to the "Pious" Williamses—"Pious" because they produced two clerics, Peyton and John Page, as well as attorney Fielding, ambassador Murat, physician Armistead Dandridge, and businessman Richard. And two Williams daughters married clergymen.

A streak of unexpected liberalism runs through the "Pious" Lewis Williams clan, which stresses good deeds and the Ten Commandments. Unlike most old Richmond families, most of these Williamses are Democrats, who prefer the liberal gospel of the *Washington Post* to the conservative one of the *Times-Dispatch*. (Most wealthy "old Richmonders" are now Republicans.)

Close kin to the Langbourne Williams descendants are the Carrington and Walter Williamses—the "Medical Williamses," who descend from William Williams, the first Langbourne's brother. They tend to be surgeons, including the two brothers I knew in Richmond—Carrington, Jr., and Armistead Marshall Williams.

A totally different Williams clan was that of tobacconist Thomas Williams and his brother, Adolphus D., known in his life as A. D. or "Aydie." They are the "Tobacco Williamses."

Richmond Newspapers

Preservationist Mary Wingfield Scott lays her own bricks after buying handsome 19th-century Linden Row on Franklin Street, now a hotel.

They're notable because T. C., a Baptist, endowed the University of Richmond law school and developed Windsor Farms around his West End house, called Agecroft. Equally important, A. D. and his wife left the Virginia Museum in 1952 their collection of fine paintings and money to buy others.

Of all the Williamses, the most sensational was the first John Skelton, of the "Railroad Williams" clan. His founding of the Seaboard Railway in Richmond in 1900 made him a business mogul at 34. Soon President Woodrow Wilson named him Comptroller of the Currency, thus enabling little Richmond in 1913 to wrest the Fifth Federal Reserve headquarters away from Baltimore—a boost to Richmond's wealth and ego.

The most intellectual of Richmond's WASP dynasties, the Williamses increasingly favor academic and professional careers. Daughters are becoming lawyers. What next?

The local standing of the Valentine family rests partly on the mercantile success of Mann Satterwhite Valentine (1824–1892), who kept a store in Richmond and originated Valentine's therapeutic meat juice, and partly on the artistry of his brother, sculptor Edward Virginius Valentine (1838–1930). It was Mann who gave his house, his art and Virginia Indian artifacts, and a princely $50,000 to create one of America's first civic museums, the Valentine Museum of Richmond History.

To this, his brother, sculptor "Eddie," helped out with gifts of his sculpture models and drawings. After this start, Richmonders have pitched in and given pictures, books, furniture, clothes, and mementos galore. As a result, few cities have such a complete museum of their past as Richmond.

Emigrant Jacob Valentine (not a WASP himself, though he and his descendants married WASPs), came to King William County in 1754 as a Huguenot from France. It was his grand-

Richmond Newspapers

The garden of the Wickham Valentine house survives from Victorian times. It was once the garden of sculptor Edward Virginius Valentine, called "Uncle Eddie."

Virginia Historical Society

Edward Virginius Valentine, Richmond sculptor, left money and art to create the Valentine Museum. Here he reads in the sculpture studio amid his works.

son, the first Mann, who moved to Richmond in 1806 and opened a dry goods store while managing the new state penitentiary. The second Mann (1824–1892) enlarged the store and created the museum on Clay Street after living many years in the Wickham house next door. Twice married, Mann II had ten children. From them have come lawyers, bankers, merchants, and others.

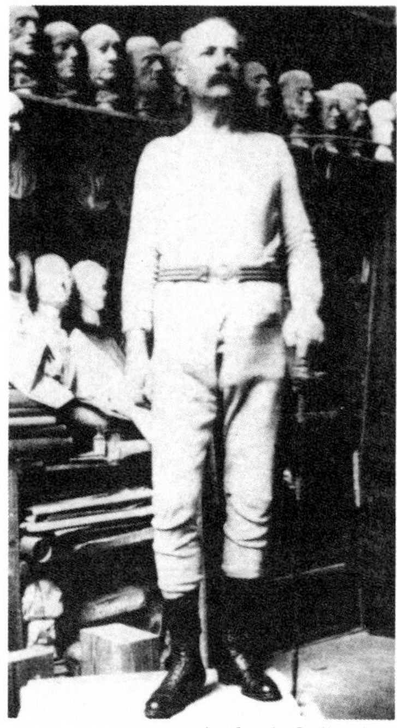

Author's Collection

Robert E. Lee, Jr., called "Rooney," posed in underwear for sculptor Edward Virginius Valentine to sculpt a statue of his father for the Capitol in Washington.

More artistic than most WASP dynasties, the Valentines today are mighty proud of "Uncle Eddie" and his sculptures. They should be. In his career, Edward Virginius Valentine studied anatomy in Richmond and then studied under European sculptors of his day. After the Civil War he specialized in sculpting Confederate heroes, giving Richmond a wealth of heroic statuary in its museums and elsewhere. He was also the sculptor of the recumbent statue of Lee at Washington and Lee.

Though smaller and less rich than other dynasties, the Valentines showed foresight in starting a museum while Richmond was still mired in the Civil War's aftermath. What's more, Mann and Edward V. Valentine made their gifts before Uncle Sam permitted tax deductibility for such gifts.

~ ~ ~

When *Town and Country* published a Richmond issue in 1951, it asked Maria Williams Sheerin—one of the "Pious" Williamses—to describe Richmond's WASP dynasties. She began by conjuring up the vision of a typical Richmond business board of a century or more ago:

> In the early part of the 19th century, four men arrived in Richmond. They wore the black stocks and "gates ajar" collars of their day and looked around at the First Families and told them to move over. Their names were Mr. Valentine, Mr. Bryan, Mr. Scott, and Mr. Williams. . . .
>
> At the hypothetical meeting of city planners which gave the city a shot in the arm in the early 1800s, four members of the hypothetical board were named. Mr. Valentine became secretary and historian; Mr. Scott, chairman of the finance committee; Mr. Bryan chairman of the committee on public relations; and Mr. Williams chairman on population.
>
> They were talented men and worked diligently at everything connected with the development of the town. Today there are few people who remember that they were ever newcomers. . . .

Fictional though that explanation may be, it confirms a truth which WASP dynasts are reluctant to admit: today's wealthy Richmonders were yesterday's poor immigrants. In a society that depends on the rise of the energetic, there's always room at the top, even in Waspish Richmond.

Virginia Historical Society

Valentine's statue of Jefferson lent dignity to the Hotel Jefferson, but visitors paid more attention to live alligators in the lobby.

10

Sweet-Scented Main Street

THE JAMES brings both gain and pain to Richmond. Over the years, coal, produce, and manufactured goods from the upcountry came down its canal to Richmond, there to be sold or shipped down the lower James for Atlantic or foreign ports. At George Washington's urging, Virginia in the 1790s built the canal around impassible stretches of the river to move tobacco and wheat downstream.

But the James can also betray the city, as when spring or autumn rains flood the river and bring tons of silt whirling down its narrow banks. When that happens, it inundates waterside buildings and fields, raising the water level at Richmond to overflow into Main, Byrd, and other downtown streets. Fortunately, floodwalls have now been built.

The canal boats ended their life with the Civil War. The old

Author's Collection

Buyers for cigarette companies examine tobacco at auction in Richmond. Since World War II, the market has moved south, much of it to North Carolina.

tow path used by horses along the canal was bought by the Chesapeake and Ohio Railroad, and the Age of Heavy Industry invaded Richmond. Alas, the river now plays only a small role in business.

When I first alighted at Richmond and walked up Main Street, I breathed the alluring odor of tobacco, which for centuries has perfumed Richmond's downtown. It came from factories that lay between Main Street's "Tobacco Road" and the canal that paralleled the James, flowing east from Bosher's Dam to Rockett's Landing in downtown Richmond.

The James and its deep-water docks once shipped thousands of hogsheads of Virginia's Sweet-Scented and Orinoco tobaccos overseas, before the Civil War fragmented the canal and before railroads came in to replace it. Today the river is almost dead except for newsprint, gravel, and petroleum shipments.

But tobacco is still Richmond's distinctive product, just as the cod is Boston's. It gives the city a character that transcends the 20th century's impersonal expressways.

Richmond was once the "tobacco capital," but it has given way to rivals in North Carolina and Kentucky. Even so, its bright leaf belt still extends from the James River at Richmond southward across the Carolinas to Georgia. Buyers fan out each fall from Richmond to follow the market in warehouses southward through Petersburg, South Boston, Danville, and the Carolinas. Much of it is bought for cigarettes to be exported or to be manufactured abroad because of the mildness of Virginia tobacco.

I became acquainted with Main Street as the center of tobacco factories, banks, and law firms. A lot of news is made there, in courtrooms, banks and law offices. The tobacco factories were first built in Richmond's early years near Rocketts on the James, named for a long-ago ferryman. They now adjoin the abandoned canal, which once received barges laden with tobacco from the upcountry, pulled eastward by the river current. Some of the 19th-century factories are now condos.

No longer visible in downtown Richmond is the canal's disused turning basin, where barges turned around after unloading, to be towed by horses back upstream to Lynchburg or Lexington; it now lies beneath skyscrapers in the downtown James Center. Some barges once came downstream all the way from Thomas Jefferson's Monticello, guided by slaves down the Fluvanna until it joined the James. At its 19th-century height, the canal reached from Richmond west to Buchanan in Botetourt County.

A Richmond barber told me a Main Street story I've never forgotten. Mr. Billy Frazier was an important local businessman, who continued to drive a Ford to work despite his success. One day a Cadillac salesman invaded his office to give him a sales pitch.

"Mr. Frazier, a man in your position can't afford to drive down Main Street in a Ford," he said in conclusion.

"Young man," replied Frazier, looking him in the eye, "a man in my position can afford to drive down Main Street on a *jackass* if he so desires! Good day, sir!"

Lower Main was Richmond's Wall Street, with banks and brokerages scowling behind granite facades in an urban canyon. All of Richmond's banks were locally owned in my newspaper days, but changed State laws since World War II have permitted them to merge into chains, headquartered in Richmond, Charlotte, and Northern Virginia.

The prowess of North Carolina bankers was often remarked in Richmond. Today, after the General Assembly has permitted chain banking, most of Richmond's large banks have formed interstate conglomerates. Charlotte has taken the lead over Richmond as a regional banking center.

"Southside," as Virginians call the area south and west of Richmond and the James, plays a quiet part in Virginia life. Rural and old-fashioned, it depends on the *Times-Dispatch* for tobacco-belt news and ads of stores. Once in Richmond, Southside shoppers made a bee-line for Miller and Rhoads and Thalhimers, lunching at the Miller and Rhoads tea room while fashion models paraded and Eddie Weaver played the organ.

The tea room was the favorite meeting place for in-towners and out-of-towners. Originally a ladies' sanctuary, it grew so popular that a men's section was added. For very little money, you could get an excellent devilled crab with tomato aspic or your date could order a frozen fruit salad with finger sandwiches. Meanwhile, good-looking models like Sue Neal and Lucy Gordon Smith kept parading between dining tables, making small talk and showing off clothes.

A day's outing in Richmond was a treat for rural folk. In mid-afternoon, before starting home to Emporia or Boydton, out-of-town shoppers just had to stop at White's on Grace Street for a ritual hot fudge sundae. Nobody made tastier chocolates than White's. Or maybe the visitors enjoyed a matinee at Loew's Theatre on the northeast corner of Grace and Sixth Streets. Built like a rococo Moorish palace, Loew's exhibited a cloud ceiling with twinkling stars above its Italianate grandeur. Eddie Weaver played the organ and invited the audience to sing along with him, following the rhythm of a ball that bounced over lyrics on the screen.

We bachelors chortled at a Loew's ad showing bosomy Jane Russell half-naked, with the message, "All the Big Ones Come to Loew's."

~ ~ ~

Much of the city's industry lay in South Richmond—the onetime Manchester, annexed in 1910. Petersburg Pike, which crossed the James in downtown Richmond, was the main artery to such old-fashioned Southside counties as Chesterfield, Amelia, Dinwiddie, Nottoway, Prince Edward, Brunswick, Lunenburg, and Mecklenburg. Once Virginians

Virginia Historical Society

Whiskey was sold by keg in pre-Prohibition Richmond. Householders and saloons bought it from Julien Binford grocery store.

called them "The Black Belt" for their heavy black population, but the racial designation was avoided after segregation became an issue.

~ ~ ~

Richmond newspaper readers in my day cherished news stories of the large estates left by rich men and women when they died, then usually published in newspapers but later halted out of respect to the wishes of decedents. When businessman Claiborne Gooch died at his home on Three Chopt Road, the *Times-Dispatch* front-paged his estate of over $20 millions. His brother in Lynchburg, who was surprised at the sum, was quoted as saying, "Why, ol' Claiborne didn't even have a good huntin' dog."

~ ~ ~

Richmond's top local tobacconist when I came to town was Larus and Brothers, on Main Street. When employees struck in the 1940s, Larus fought back. Strikes were rare in Richmond, so the newspapers front-paged the Larus strike daily. I covered the conflict, hustling down Main Street to cross the picket line and talk with union leaders and with Bob Carden, Larus's embattled manager.

Anti-New Deal Richmonders blamed the strike on Franklin D. Roosevelt's labor policies, but it went deeper than that. The company's chief products in my day were Domino cigarettes, retailed at ten cents per pack and smoked by both poor and well-to-do-folk, and Edgeworth pipe tobacco, smoked by Josef Stalin.

Richmonders economized on tobacco and whiskey. Most of them then drank cheap blends and smoked Dominos. "If you drink and smoke as much as I do," one State senator told me, "all the damned stuff tastes the same."

~ ~ ~

Despite Jefferson's advocacy of wine, Richmonders of the 1940s stuck to whiskey, which had been outlawed in Virginia in 1914. By agreement between Senator Byrd and Bishop

Colonial Williamsburg

Cock-fighting is a popular sport around Richmond, especially south of the James where fights are held secretly. It is against the law.

James Cannon, the Methodist prohibitionist czar of Virginia, ardent spirits were permitted to return in the 1930s at first only in State-run ABC bottle stores. Not until after Byrd retired were mixed drinks sold again in Virginia.

During Prohibition, Virginians could get a bottle of bourbon monthly if certified as a medical need. Many recipients signed for their bottles in drugstore records as "James Cannon" or as "Fulmer Bright," Richmond's anti-whiskey mayor.

Cannon's role in Virginia politics was criticized by most non-Methodists, and many jokes were made. *Times-Dispatch* cartoonist Fred Seibel ridiculed him in a famous cartoon, "But When Does the Bishop Bish?"

Virginia had had several distilleries before Prohibition, but none revived after it ended. However, the Smith Bowman Distilleries opened in Northern Virginia in the 1930s to make Virginia Gentleman and Fairfax County bourbon. The monthly arrival of hard-to-get Virginia Gentleman in State ABC stores during the whiskey rationing of World War II was awaited impatiently by tipplers. One ABC store clerk told his minister after church each Sunday when his brand was in stock. In Richmond, a leading businessman came to blows in an ABC store with a newcomer who insisted on sharing the store's limited supply of Virginia Gentleman.

I found Richmond full of beguiling antique and secondhand book shops. One day I spotted a Victorian coffee service in an old store, and bought it for $3. Its silver plate was engraved "Anthony and Sons," which I learned was a saloon that had flourished at Sixth and Broad Streets—on "the wrong side of Broad."

The Anthonys had operated saloons in the wide-open days, before Bishop Cannon and his minions dried up Virginia.

One of their pubs was the Commercial Hotel at 912 East Main Street, whose window was lettered, "Lynnhaven Bay Oysters." Hung outside each morning was a display of wild game. Specialties were venison, partridge, and quail. Alas, Virginia in 1914 also restricted the sale of wild game for health reasons, putting both the Anthonys' wild-game restaurant and saloons out of business.

Even so, the brothers didn't surrender. They moved to cigarmaking as a substitute. Richmonders remember the father as Albert Gallatin Anthony and his sons as Al Junior, Frank, James, and John Henry. My wife and I gave our Anthony saloon coffee set to James Anthony, Jr.

~ ~ ~

The cruel sport of cock-fighting was still much alive south of the James around Richmond. As a reporter, I heard of bloody Saturday-night specials held in old barns or tobacco warehouses in Southside, where aficionados would bring their little red and black roosters, in fighting trim for high-stakes combat. It's a man's sport, for most women can't stand the sight of the bleeding combatants, fighting to the death with steel spurs. With these, the cocks try to cut each other to death brought on by blood letting.

Because of its cruelty, cock-fighting is prohibited, but Southside and Piedmont residents still pursue it on the q.t. But watch out for the police.

~ ~ ~

In the automobile era of the 1920s, Richmond turned its back on the James. However, in my years there, interest in the river and canal began to revive. Once the canal had extended from Richmond northwestward through Chesterfield, Powhatan, Cumberland, Goochland, Fluvanna, Buchanan, Nelson,

Amherst, and Bedford counties to the mountains. Packet service was provided by narrow vessels up to 100 feet long and only 15 or 20 feet wide. Passengers sat and dined in good weather on an open deck and went below nightly to bathe and sleep, the sexes separated only by a curtain.

Wrote journalist George W. Bagby of a canal trip from Richmond to his former home in Lynchburg:

> The packet landing at the foot of Eighth Street presented a scene of great activity. . . . At last we were off, slowly pushed under the bridge at Seventh Street; then the horses were hitched; then slowly along, until at length, with a lively jerk as the horses fell into a trot, away we went, the cutwater throwing the spray as we rounded the Penitentiary Hill, and the passengers lingered on deck to get a last look at the fair city of Richmond. . . .
>
> There was abundant leisure to enjoy the scenery, that grew more and more captivating as we rose, lock after lock, into the rock-bound eminences of the upper James. . . . The bar was small, but vigorous and healthy. . . . 'Gentlemen, your very good health.'; 'Colonel, my respects to you.'; 'My regards, Judge.'
>
> After supper, we talked and smoked on deck while women played cards and sewed. Gamblers were avoided. At bedtime a curtain was drawn across the lower-deck saloon to separate the quarters of men and women. Berths were stacked three high.

The canal was doomed not only by the arrival of the railroad age but also by the inherent frailty of canal locks. Spring rains repeatedly flooded the James, crushing the locks and filling the canal bottom. An 1870 print from *Harper's Weekly* depicted a James River flood rising over the steps of Richmond's Main Street stores. On the Maury River in Lexington, the same 1870 flood washed away the wooden coffin being built for Robert E. Lee's interment. In the huge flood, trees and dead cows floated downstream and were caught on Richmond's rocks.

Virginia Historical Society

Lower Main was repeatedly submerged when James River overflowed. This scene is from Frank Leslie's newspaper of December 15, 1877. The flooding has continued till recently.

~ ~ ~

By the time I moved to Richmond in 1940, steamboat service from Richmond to Norfolk was ending for lack of passengers and freight. As a boy, though, I had seen the last of the steamers, *Pocahontas,* chugging past my home in Newport News and disappearing toward Richmond, beneath the lift of the James River drawbridge. By that time the *Pocahontas* hauled mostly freight, for the day-long trip was too slow for most passengers.

The sooty white vessel stopped at a dozen towns and plantation docks on the James—Newport News, Jamestown, Hopewell, Westover, Berkeley, and Shirley among them. Dock owners with cargo or passengers beckoned the *Pocahontas* in by hoisting a white flag. Dock masters often served also as rural postmasters.

Shad and herring abounded until the 1940s, and I saw Main Street factory workers at lunchtime on the river shore, scooping up the herring and shad in long-handled nets. The fish fought their way up the rocky river to spawn. Shad season in March was foretold by the white blossoms on the shadbush along the river.

Slim Speight, a friend of mine who ran a parking lot on "the wrong side" of Broad Street, each year held a shad bake for the Governor and other good ol' boys at the Hotel Richmond. Occasionally he substituted chitterlings for devotees of that rural delicacy. The term "good ol' boy," wasn't yet current in the 1940s, but it aptly describes Virginians like Slim, bred in the country and devoted to huntin', fishin', and outdoor urination.

You can be a WASP and a good ol' boy at the same time, as Slim Speight showed me. It helps if you own a hunting dog and a farm in the country. The breeding and skill of your dog are important measures of your Waspness and of your standing in your hunt club. Virginians can tell a gentleman by his dogs.

Author's Collection

Billboards flourished on roadsides in the 1940s. At Bartlett's in Southside stood this unpainted cabin advertising Camels and patent medicine.

The Army's Fort Lee near Petersburg grew to be a city of its own in the war, and Richmond became a liberty town for its homesick GIs. They thronged Saturday night dances at the Mosque and at USO headquarters on Grace Street. Others preferred the lurid offerings of Hortense Blair's Willow Works before Uncle Sam shut her down.

Honkytonks also flourished on Petersburg Pike, not far from Lady Wonder, "The Talking Horse." Everywhere they went, GIs and dates had to take their own Four Roses or Old Guckenheimer in a brown bag and hide it from the bouncer. After the Army closed Hortense Blair and other carnal palaces, the girls became street-walkers or "masseuses." Boys will be boys. And girls girls. Even in Waspish Richmond.

The lonely farmland of Southside Virginia, south of the James from Richmond, has stayed with me ever since my childhood. It is a land of farms and pine forests, knit together by narrow roads and sprinkled with indolent courthouse towns. I later put my reminiscences of the area into a book, *Below the James Lies Dixie,* summing up those impressions in these stanzas:

Cypress standin' in the Dismal Swamp,
Full moon shinin' on the corn,
Log fires burnin' in the old smokehouse
There in ol' Virginia I was born

Blackbirds flockin' roun' the peanut vines,
Tobacco brownin' in the sun,
Rooster crowin' in the cotton patch,
Banjo music when work's done.

(chorus)

Below the James lies Dixie,
The lan' God made for me
Where the pines grow tall and catbirds call
And the fields stretch far as you can see.
Below the James lies Dixie,
Where August comes to stay,
And the world moves slow while the collards grow
Down in Dixie, U.S.A.

Sunset shinin' on the River James,
Hoot owl cryin' in the trees,
Dear old southland where I once was young,
Pine boughs swayin' in the breeze.

Bright eyes sparklin' in the golden dusk,
Warm hearts callin' me to come.
Nighttime fallin', and I've got to go
Below the old James River to my home.

(chorus)

Below the James lies Dixie
The land God made for me,
Where the pines grow tall and the catbirds call
And fields stretch far as you can see.
Below the James lies Dixie
Where August comes to stay,
And the world moves slow while the collards grow,
Down in Dixie, U.S.A.

11

The Club, the Beach, the Rivah

IN THE SOCIAL SHORTHAND of Richmond, natives spoke of "the Club," "the Beach," and "the Rivah." Outsiders were supposed to know automatically that natives referred to the Country Club of Virginia, the resort city of Virginia Beach, and the fringed shoreline of Tidewater where city folk fled on summer weekends. It made young Richmonders feel important to talk like that.

A fourth Richmond lodestar was "the University," which of course meant Charlottesville. But we scholars from Washington and Lee resisted this as presumptuous. W&L auto stickers claimed that "Washington and Lee is THE University of Virginia." My fellow alumnus, Charley McDowell, used to put down our Charlottesville nemesis as "State U."

Parochial as it may be, a few compass points defined the

world of contented Richmonders in the 1940s. They spent their winter at "the University," their summer at "the Beach" or "the Rivah," and their Saturday nights at "the Club." Who could ask for anything more?

I got elected to the Country Club of Virginia, buying a $500 share of stock (it is now worth $20,000) so I could enjoy the swimming pool (Lake Urine) and the Saturday night dances to a live band. Most young men took dates, changing partners by cutting in on the dance floor, but others went just to look on. Those were the days of the foxtrot, the waltz, and the rhumba, but jitterbugging was beginning to liven things up. Stags like Hartwell "Harpy" Reed would survey the dance floor from the sidelines and then cut in on you just when you didn't want him to.

Each male carried his own pint or quart of bourbon or blended whiskey, hidden in a paper bag because it was against the law to consume liquor publicly. We mixed it with Coca Cola or had the bartender make a whiskey sour. A few avant-gardes drank Scotch or gin, but vodka was yet unheard of. Between dances we sat around tables and talked about the draft. You saw the same faces each Saturday, around the same tables—old-timers at some and newcomers at others, while elderly lady chaperons in the balcony watched the goings-on.

At midnight the band played "Goodnight, Sweetheart" and the house lights flickered. Time to go home. That was the era of blue laws, when Sunday revels and labor were prohibited. By Richmond's reckoning, you should rest up for Sunday school and church. Nowadays all that seems very childish, but I'm not sure it wasn't better that way.

Another club was the Deep Run Hunt, which sat amid green meadows in Goochland County, where many of Richmond's commuters now live. I got to know the club through Jack Sands, who wrote its history, and Major Murray Bayliss, RAF, a garrulous Irish daredevil who married a Richmond girl (the daughter of Victor Williams of the Lawyer Williams clan) and built a house, Fox Hill, in the horse country west of Richmond.

Bayliss—his full moniker was William Murray Forbes Bayliss—spent most of World War II in the Royal Air Force. He was an Errol Flynn sort of guy with a guardsman's mustache, a naughty sense of humor, and a willingness to say or do anything. After the war, he founded the weekly *Goochland Gazette,* where his column, "Looking Backwards," spoke out on everything. Nobody could censor Murray Bayliss.

As MFH at Goochland, Murray kept British equine traditions alive in Virginia's capital. (He also kept beagles and called himself "the beaglah.") The club put on the Deep Run races, at Curles Neck in Henrico, later moved to Strawberry Hill. There you could see the Major, handsome in pinks, astride his horse. At race meets you'd hear the Major's veddy British cry, "Tally ho! The fawx!"

In old age Murray Bayliss unveiled his bizarre career in a memoir, *Out in the Midday Sun.* He told of the time in World War II when he stirred up a hive of bees beneath the seats of a German officers' latrine. Later, as a German war prisoner, he was interviewed by Joachim von Ribbentrop, Hitler's foreign minister. And on a trip through Afghanistan's mountains on a pack pony, he was invited to sleep with his choice of the chieftain's daughters.

"Unhappily, I felt compelled to refuse," he reported. "The girls smelled perfectly frightful, a combination of rancid butter, goat, and badger."

Returning to England by ship from India, he became the Aga Khan's nightly bridge partner and with the Aga won nearly $5,000. The Major and his P. G. Wodehouse mannerisms ("I say there, my good man") are greatly missed at the Deep Run Hunt. I can hear him even now proclaiming, "Tally ho! The fawx."

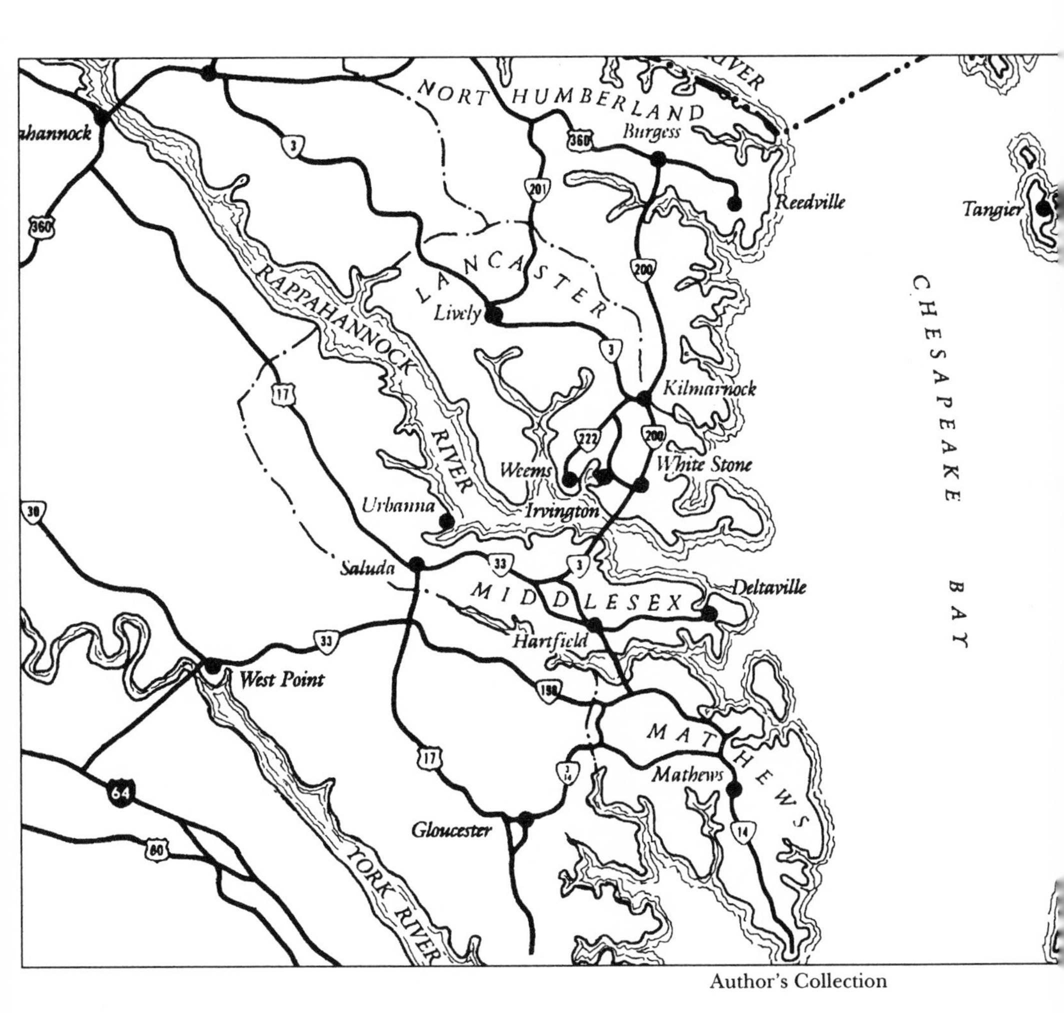

Author's Collection

The auto enabled city folk to drive on weekends to vacation cottages they built along waterways. Douglas Freeman called it "the Virginia Riviera."

~ ~ ~

I had spent summers when I grew up on my grandparents' Isle of Wight farm, but I was ignorant of race horses; I didn't know the paddocks from the buttocks, so to speak. I was amused at the races one day when the announcer proclaimed over the loudspeaker system: "The judges have just scratched Mrs. Whitney's Fuzzy-Wuzzy." I presume Liz Whitney was not amused.

~ ~ ~

When automobiles came in with World War I, Richmonders began to buy vacation houses along the Chesapeake's waterways–those "rivahs" they talked about. Weekends at the river became stylish, made possible by new bridges and ferries throughout Tidewater. Dr. Freeman in his broadcasts glorified the region as "Virginia's Riviera," often predicting on Friday, "It's going to be a glorious weekend on Virginia's Riviera!"

Doctors were the first to find these weekend hideaways, to get away from their patients' phone calls. At one time, Gloucester County alone was the weekend retreat of Doctors Frank Johns, Morrison Hutcheson, Claude Coleman, Page Mauck, Norton Mason, and Finley Gayle, Jr. An hour's drive from Richmond brought you a choice of the James, York, Mattaponi, Pamunkey, Rappahannock, or Chesapeake. By today's prices, water frontage was then cheap.

Colonies developed as one buyer in turn attracted another. Families left Richmond in the new Dodge or Oldsmobile on Friday afternoon, taking the cook, and returned Sunday afternoon, tired but happy. Early maid's rooms were later converted to pantries. The family soon learned to cope with a Delco generator, a sailboat called a "Sharpy," outdoor cook-outs, and stinging nettles. Swimming pools came later.

A typical Richmond summer colony was Gloucester Banks on the York. One day in 1923, Mr. and Mrs. George Morgan of Richmond found themselves at Gloucester Point, awaiting Captain Willie Ashe's ferry, *Cornwallis.* Gazing up, they were struck by the view across the York to Yorktown. "What a lovely place for a summer colony," said Mrs. Morgan, and they bought it.

By 1924 Morgan and nineteen associates had enough partners signed up to hire Edwin Conquest, a civil engineer just out of VMI, to lay out lots and boss workmen in felling trees, dressing them into lumber, and building 20 cottages. They called it Gloucester Banks.

The group extended a long pier into the York and created a netted swimming area to fend off stinging nettles, a bane of Virginia's tidal waters. For years, until the 1970s, cottagers depended on one public phone, placed inconveniently in the caretaker's cottage. (They *didn't want* to get calls.) Cottagers used their summer places from Memorial Day through Labor Day. (Richmonders move like lemmings.) All have since been greatly improved and have descended to a third or fourth generation, but few have been sold. Some outsiders call the lifestyle incestuous.

Like many Richmond vacation places, "Little Richmond," as the natives call it, on the York is plain as an old shoe, but WASPs seem to prefer it that way. Similar summer cottages today line many tidal waterways of Virginia.

Life on Virginia's Riviera in no way resembled the topless bathing to be found on the real Riviera in France. It was much the same quiet routine as at Gwynn's Island on the Piankatank, at Sandy Point on the Potomac, or at Cobb's Creek in Mathews. A few rowboats were visible at the shoreline and a few sailboats or power boats at anchor offshore. Activities were simple and usually innocent.

Fishing was good in those years, and anglers reeled in croakers and spot by handline; rods and reels came later, when the fish had all but disappeared. Crabbing by handline was replaced in the 1940s by crab pots, invented by a New England emigré to Virginia who simply adapted the lobster pot. Baited with oily fish and dropped to the bottom with a rope and Clorox plastic float, the wire mesh pot overnight collects crabs. The pots have become endemic along Virginia's Riviera.

Richmond Newspapers

Skirts were long and bathing suits modest when Tides Inn was opened by Ennolls Stephens at Irvington. The auto made waterfront weekends popular in Richmond.

Weekday steamers served Tidewater rivers until World War II, when I worked in Richmond. The boat's daily arrival with passengers, mail, and freight at docks like New Point Light, Kilmarnock, Urbanna, and White Stone, attracted a daily gathering. At Gloucester Point, Richmonders could come and go by a steamer which stopped also at West Point, Clay Bank, Old Point, and Norfolk.

Young hell-raisers at Gloucester Banks at night drank Coca Colas at Spencer Clopton's pier house and danced to his jukebox. Hits like "I'll Be Seeing You" and "The White Cliffs of Dover" reminded you we were at war. (Can't you hear them now?)

Every summer colony should have its hang-out like Spencer Clopton's. In his refrigerator Spencer kept soft drinks and live bait for fishermen—soft crabs, peelers, and bloodworms. After awhile the soft crabs tasted like Coca Colas and the Cokes like soft crabs. Each cost ten cents.

Some Richmonders went north in summer to Squam, Winnepesaukee, Kennebunkport, Fisher's Island, or Martha's Vineyard, but Virginia Beach was *the* place for young Richmond during World War II. The Cavalier Beach Club was the favorite stomping ground of wartime Richmonders and other low country Virginians. Looking out over the moonswept Atlantic, Hal Kemp's band made magic music. The club's popularity attracted the competition of the rival Surf Club for awhile. Around the two, at night in the sand dunes and the sea oats, service men and their girls made the most of their last days together. Nobody seemed to mind.

In those days Virginia Beach hotels were family affairs, run as boarding-houses by ladies like Miss Lemoine of the Albemarle or Mrs. Sterling of the Princess Anne. Families would

Tides Inn

Ennolls and Anne Stephens, at center, opened Tides Inn in 1946. Its bar challenged guests to drink from 17th-century Dutch "wager cups."

stay weeks at a time, eating huge meals between swims. The bourbon bottle and the water pitcher were passed on the porch at coctail hour. The last of the "cottages," the Avamere and the Halifax, were torn down in the mid-nineties to make way for high-rise hotels.

The war hit Virginia Beach one Saturday in 1941, shortly before Pearl Harbor. While thousands looked on, a merchant ship offshore suffered an underwater explosion and sank in sight of the crowd. Was it torpedoed by a German submarine? Military planes combed the area, but no sub was found. The damage had been done by a mine planted days earlier by a German U-boat, which had crept close to shore one night.

One of the children playing on the beach at the time of the explosion was John Dalton of Radford, who would become governor of Virginia from 1978 to 1982. The explosion brought the war closer to all of us in Virginia than anything before it.

Next day I went up to Lombardy Street in Richmond and renewed my application for an officer's commission in the Navy.

Richmonders weren't the only ones to discover the pleasure of Virginia's shore. In 1944 a native of Northumberland County, Ennolls Stephens, of New Orleans, bought 23 acres in Lancaster around the Rappahannock and built the Tides Inn as a golf and waterside resort. "Big Steve" had made a fortune in New Oleans auto dealerships and radio stations, but he was homesick for his Northern Neck. He was one of five Virginia brothers, another being A. E. S. "Gi" (for "Giant") Stephens, of Smithfield, who was lieutenant governor after World War II.

Strengthening his ties to the Northern Neck, "Steve" Stephens had married Anne Lee, daughter of fisheries commissioner McDonald Lee, and the couple exuded charm and energy. Their Tides Inn and Tides Lodge became top resorts and attracted droves of retirees. Richmonders flocked to live there after the war.

Roads from Richmond to the Rivah in the 1940s were chock-a-block with Richmonders every summer weekend. In those years when a two-lane highway served most areas, traffic had to crawl to Yorktown to board Captain Ashe's tiny ferry.

After the 1933 hurricane, the Yorktown and Gloucester ferry docks had to be moved and rebuilt. Bigger ferries were needed to handle the traffic.

Authors Collection

Richmonders formed an unfavorable view of Newport News from trips down Route 60 to the ferry across Hampton Roads, headed for Virginia Beach.

The ferry from Yorktown docked at Gloucester Point, near Spencer Clopton's "confectionery," and the Gloucester road wound past daffodil fields and ancient churches. One sign read, "Fred Wants To See You Dance," and another, "Madame Clara, Palmist." But the Burma-Shave rhymes were the best, selling shaving cream in iambic pentameter.

Realtors assigned Gloucester's rivers a pecking order determined by land prices. At the top stood North River, then the Ware, the East, Mobjack Bay, and Wilson Creek. My own choice was the York itself. Dick Talley dubbed Gloucester Banks on the York "The Greenwich Village of Gloucester," but, much as I liked the Banks, they seemed too tame to be a Riviera. Richmond WASPs aren't given to topless bathing or most other public display. They'd only skinny dip at night when the moon is low.

Tidewater families long ago took their children out of town in August to avoid "the dog days," which the dictionary defines as "the sultry part of summer, when Sirius, the Dog Star, rises at the same time as the sun." Virginia's summer spas sprang up after colonial times, beginning with Berkeley Springs, now in West Virginia. Few survive as watering places except Hot Springs, Warm Springs, and Orkney in Virginia, and Berkeley and White Sulphur in West Virginia.

Nobody any longer fears "dog days," but wealthy and old-fashioned Richmonders still enjoy the springs, both in summer and for winter sports. They call them "The Hot," "The Warm," and "The White." Cottagers at Hot Springs like to remember the glorious days when Douglas Fairbanks, Jr., and his West Virginia-born wife had a cottage there.

Richmonders didn't think much of my hometown of Newport News or of Norfolk. They based their impressions on what they saw of Newport News on their way down Route 60 to the Newport News Boat Harbor ferry and thence across Hampton Roads to Norfolk. In Newport News the route led down raffish Jefferson Avenue, with many vacant stores and sidewalk idlers visible.

"Do *nice* people *live* in Newport News?" Richmonders teased me. I reminded them that Jesus lived in Nazareth, which was no Garden of Eden, either.

12

Spielers and Spellbinders

WHEN THE BRYANS' *News Leader* moved to its new plant on Fourth Street in the 1930s, before I arrived in Richmond, Dr. Freeman as editor stopped the work force in the lobby of the newly opened building and asked them to kneel in prayer for their fine new quarters.

Ink-stained reporters and churlish printers couldn't believe their ears. "Most of them had never prayed," said *Times-Dispatch* State Editor Dick Carter, who remembered it. "They didn't know how. But the Doc was a dyed-in-the-wool Baptist preacher, and he took over. Had 'em all down on hands and knees."

Then as now, Richmond was a church-oriented city. When newcomers complained that Richmond was aloof, Dr. Freeman wrote an editorial saying they should join a church and get to know God and their neighbors. Richmond's life began with churches, he said, and indeed the city had fine preachers and church buildings.

Unlike the Baptists and Methodists in Newport News, I found Richmond dominated by Episcopalians and Presbyterians. They were its most influential congregations, from St. Paul's on Capitol Square to St. Stephen's ("Saint Convenience"), built in the West End boondocks in the 1920s and now engulfed in suburban traffic. Preachers like Churchill Gibson of St. James' were constantly quoted. Richmonders liked to go to church, especially to big funerals.

I was surprised to find so much rivalry among congregations. St. Paul's was called "arrogant" by other churchmen. St. Stephen's was said by other Episcopalians to be full of warmed-over Baptists. One rival vestryman called Grace and Holy Trinity "the first church of the second families." Dr. Blanton Belk, minister of St. Giles' Presbyterian, was thought by some to be theologically liberal. ("Liberal" in Richmond meant unsound.)

Certainly St. Paul's on the Square was the most controversial congregation. It usually chose outspoken rectors who voiced views more advanced than their flock's. It was said that the ideal rector for St. Paul's would be a liberal preacher and pastor who was a Confederate veteran not over forty.

Mrs. Beverley Randolph Wellford didn't care for women's assumption of men's roles at St. Paul's. "Nowadays," she told me in Richmond, "I find myself ushered into St. Paul's by Rossie Reed and served the holy communion by Mary Tyler Cheek. I have nothing against either one, but I want to be served the holy wafer by *a frocked priest.*"

Henry St. George Tucker of Richmond was presiding bishop of the Episcopal Church in the United States when I lived in Richmond, and I interviewed him for a Sunday feature. He was a tall, ungainly man who liked to float in an inner tube at Virginia Beach in summer, contemplating God's universe through his toes. He was clerically absent-minded, and it was said that once in an old church he confirmed a newel post, thinking it was somebody's head, meanwhile intoning:

> Defend, O Lord, this thy child
> With thy heavenly grace,
> That he may remain thine forever
> And daily increase in thy holy spirit, more and more
> Until he may come into thy heavenly kingdom.

Unable to find his ticket for the conductor on the C&O one day, Bishop Tucker was reassured by the ticket collector, "Oh, that's all right, Reverend. I'm sure you bought one."

"It's not all right at all," Bishop Tucker is said to have replied. "Now I don't know where I'm going!"

In his readable *Hodge Podge 1*, Richmonder Joseph Bryan III relates that the Bishop was tone deaf but "joined in every hymn, always singing it to the tune of 'There Is a Green Hill Far Away,' the only tune he could carry." To his family he was "Big Saint" and his six-foot-two son was "Little Saint."

In early years St. Paul's families paid rent for their assigned pews, as was done in churches in Europe. Having a pew close to the altar was prestigious and also helped the hard-of-hearing. When the family of broker and banker Frederic Scott grew so large it could no longer fit in one pew, one Scott got the St. Paul's vestry's permission to cut out the pew barrier and link two pews into one. That made all the Scotts equal—or, at least, as equal as Scotts can be.

Many Virginians tuned in to Douglas Freeman's Sunday inspirational talks over WRNL, broadcast from his study in his home in Byrd Park and later in the West End. His wife, the former Inez Goddin, was a lifelong Episcopalian, as were the Freeman children, Mary Tyler, Anne, and James Douglas.

Like many clerics of his day, Dr. Freeman preached in dramatic style, invoking visions of hellfire and damnation. I always thought he looked like an Italian pope. He had fine

Newport News *Daily Press*

Bill Tuck succeeded Colgate Darden, Jr. as governor. He was a fine story teller and proved a good governor.

diction and the emotional shadings of a Shakespearian actor. He explained to one inquirer that his sermon style was the "pathetic" delivery, from the Greek word "pathos," meaning "evoking a feeling of compassion or pity." He teased Mrs. Freeman by describing Episcopalians as "the last remnants of the old, broken-down plantation society."

Richmonders in those days loved sermons and church music, and I visited a few churches on Sundays to enjoy choirs and preachers. At St. James' I heard Churchill Gibson opine that "Robert E. Lee is just as much a saint of the Lord's as any saint in Christendom." He liked to console fearful sinners by telling them of his elderly lady communicant who was afraid of dying. "So am I, sister! So am I!" he assured her heartily at her bedside.

At St. Paul's I heard the eloquent Dr. Vincent Franks, who had preceded me from Lexington. Announcing his coming to town, the *Times-Dispatch* had cited his "successful mission work among students of W&L and VMI," making us undergraduates sound like African savages. Perhaps the finest pulpit orator I heard in Richmond was Dr. Theodore Adams, pastor of First Baptist Church, who was president then of the World Baptist Alliance.

Richmond remembered many other clergymen, among them Moses Hoge of Second Presbyterian and Russell Bowie of St. Paul's. Dr. Bowie was called to Grace Church in New York—one of several Richmond clergy of the pre-war era to become nationally known.

A familiar Virginia story, no doubt imaginary, was of a visit of the Archbishop of Canterbury in a Richmond household while on a preaching mission in America. While His Grace took tea with his hostess, the laundress entered and interrupted her mistress to ask, "Miz Helen, do de Archangel like his shimmies sta'ched or plain?" ("Shimmies" was Southern for chemises, or underwear.) The Archangel wanted his plain.

At another point in the afternoon's conversation, the Archbishop had occasion to mention an overzealous cleric on his staff. "Alas," said the Archangel, "Brother Throckmorton is an ahss. A consecrated ahss, mind you, but still an ahss." It sounded like a line from Oscar Wilde.

Most Richmond Episcopalians were low-church, the kind I'd grown up with, but I was surprised to encounter Latin and incense in one Richmond church. It reminded me of one high church English cleric, who was described in his obituary as "a great Anglican and a middling Christian." In one Episcopal Sunday school I visited, teenagers learned this ditty, to the tune of "God Bless America":

I am an Anglican
  I am P.E. [Protestant Episcopal]
Neither high church nor low church,
  I am Catholic and Protestant and free:

Not a Presby,
  Nor a Luth'ran,
Nor a Baptist,
  White with foam.
I am an Anglican
  Just one step from Rome.

(That wouldn't have gone over very big in Smithfield.)

As an outlander, I had a hard time getting used to Richmond's suffocating Lent. It was chiefly the creation of Episcopalians and Catholics, but other denominations were enlisted as preachers and worshippers in St. Paul's widely-attended Lenten services. As I understood it, we Christians were supposed to forego earth's pleasures during Lent to heighten our joy at Easter. It was like banging on your toe to enjoy the letup.

Society Editor Corbin Old complained every year about the paucity of parties and weddings during Lent. High church Episcopalians put everything off till after Easter. At long last came that happy morning and good times again.

The best thing about Lent, I found, was the daily noontime sermon at St. Paul's, preached by eloquent clerics. It was one of Richmond's earliest interdenominational efforts, attended by all sorts of people. St. Paul's ladies raised money with their Lenten lunches, just as their counterparts at Grace and Holy Trinity profited from their Christmas plum puddings. Some church ladies had done it for years, advancing from bus girls to waitresses. It was good to see Episcopalians work, mortifying the flesh, as it were.

Oratory throve in old Richmond, which had once thrilled to Patrick Henry in St. John's Church. In my time college presidents like Edwin Alderman of the University of Virginia, Francis Gaines of Washington and Lee, and Frederic Boatwright of the University of Richmond were known for eloquence. I discovered other gifted speakers in the General Assembly, where I listened to stem-winders like John Battle of Charlottesville and Bill Tuck of Halifax.

I was especially moved by elderly, eloquent Senator Henry Taylor Wickham, of Hanover, when he spoke on Lee's birthday one January 19 in the General Assembly and sentimentally recalled his years as a student of the general's at Washington College. The old man wept, and so did his hearers.

Many General Assemblymen were lawyers who knew how to use anecdotes to sway arguments. I remember Ashton Dovell of Williamsburg telling of the little boy who wandered into a Catholic church as the censer in long cassock was swinging the incense pot in a procession. "Hey, lady," said the boy to the censer, "your pocketbook's on fire."

Another Assembly story was Bill Tuck's account of a farmer who sold another farmer a blind mule. When the buyer complained, the seller insisted, "That mule ain't blind. He just don't give a damn."

Another story told of the proud farmer who entered his plowhorse in a race at the county fair:

"That horse won't win a race," the farmer's wife argued. "You're wasting your time."

"I know it," said the farmer, "but she'll sure meet some nice horses."

Rotund Senator Billy Wright of Tappahannock, who looked like Jiggs in the funnies, realized the humor of self-deprecation. He told how he'd long ago phoned Senator Carter Glass in Washington to ask his help for two constituents who were seeking advice in Wright's Tappahannock law office.

When Senator Glass got on the line, Billy Wright said to him, "Senator, this is your old friend, Billy Wright, from Tappahannock."

"What's that?" roared the deaf and disagreeable Glass over the long distance hookup.

"Billy Wright, from Tappahannock . . ."

After an agonizing delay, Glass shouted querulously, "Billy *Who*?, from Tappa *Where*?" You could hear it all over Tappahannock.

"I never tried that again," Billy Wright said.

Bill Tuck told a story to illustrate the need for precise wording. A rural hamlet had two Baptist churches, side by side. A visitor asked why.

"Well," explained a local resident, "Dis yere church say Pharoah's daughter *found* Moses in de bullrushes. And dat dere church say Pharoah's daughter *say* she *found* Moses in de bullrushes."

It was a useful lesson for a newspaper man.

13

Lawyers and Other Nuisances

OVER-ACHIEVERS in early Virginia became planters and built fine houses like Westover, but by the time of the Revolution many of them chose to be lawyers as well as planters. Lawyers dominated Virginia's politics from Jefferson's day onward, and they continue to do so, fortified by the examples of George Wythe, Edmund Pendleton, Peyton Randolph, John Marshall, and others. Virginia alone has six law schools–too many.

Virginia lawyers are mostly conservative, lacking the striped pants glamour of Philadelphia and New York counsel, but equally able. When I moved to Richmond, most lawyers practiced alone or in pairs, but two Richmond firms have since grown huge. One of them fattened on Dalkon Shield litigation following Robins Pharmaceutical's legal imbroglio, brought on by lawsuits of unhappy users of its intra-uterine device.

~ ~ ~

When I covered courts for the paper, the pace was leisurely. My mentor was Judge Brockenbrough Lamb, who advised the *Times-Dispatch* on libel. His motto was, "When in doubt, don't!" Though Richmond courts were more punctual than most, cases moved slowly in summer, when the Rivah beckoned. Lawyers and judges like to fish, and August was too hot to be in court. Air-conditioning has changed that.

Judge Lamb had been preceded as the *Times-Dispatch* libel lawyer by mountainous Joseph Hall, who had difficulty moving his 275-pounds in and out of the Commonwealth Club bar, where he hung out and ate joyously. He was a son of Professor J. Lesslie Hall, one of William and Mary's "Seven Wise Men." Joe Hall was a fine raconteur and eventually became president of Lawyers Title Insurance Company. To slim down, he went on a turnip salad diet, eating nothing but mountains of kale, mustard greens, and Hanover greens cooked with fatback, prepared daily in the Commonwealth Club kitchen. It did the job, but he lost his sense of humor in the process.

One of the *Times-Dispatch* reporters was Maurice Dean, who knew the Federal judges and their clerks. My own chief contacts with courts were at Henrico Courthouse, which was squeezed into a miserable Victorian edifice on Main Street, reached by trolley car.

The really newsworthy courts were the Federal Circuit and District Courts on Main Street, then trying civil rights cases arising under the New Deal. These were building up toward the Supreme Court's epic 1954 decision, Brown v. Board of Education of Topeka, Kansas, one of the most influential court rulings in world history. Tempers were rising. The South faced a social revolution.

~ ~ ~

The conduct of courts especially concerned Governor Darden, who had grown up in rural Southampton County and practiced law in Norfolk. At the University of Virginia law school he had known many men who returned from law school to their home counties, like him, to practice law as their fathers had done. But many withered on the vine for lack of stimulation, Darden said, dealing as they did with simple and routine cases. Even so, some got rich, buying up tax-delinquent rural land that few people except lawyers and judges knew to be available, at bargain prices.

"No wonder so many lawyers take to drink," Darden said. He wished it were possible for them to update their training now and then as physicians did. Today things are better. Courts and lawyers are more disciplined.

~ ~ ~

Familiar to many Virginians in those days was a Victor red-seal phonograph record by Irish-American humorist Walter Kelly, titled "The Virginian Judge." In it Kelly mimicked the proceedings of a small-town police court. He changed his voice to impersonate first a brusque judge, then his quavery bailiff, and finally the court's illiterate defendants, charged with stealing chickens and other minor offenses.

Some thought the impersonated judge was the crusty Judge John Crutchfield of Richmond, but he was actually Judge J. D. G. Brown of early Newport News, where the Irish roustabout Kelly had worked in the shipyard and run a saloon before becoming an international monologuist. To capitalize on his talent, Walter Kelly traveled vaudeville circuits throughout the world, returning to Newport News at the height of his fame and "presiding" over Judge Brown's court.

No matter how heavy the "Virginian Judge"'s docket might be, he managed to get through it by his lunchtime by cutting short defendant's testimony and rendering brief, caustic decisions. The humor was racial and cruel, but Kelly managed to inject enough warmth and common sense to make the routine hilarious.

Whenever the "judge" learned that fish were biting in the James nearby, he ended the day's hearings abruptly. "Court dismissed," he roared, banging his gavel without explanation. Today the behavior of courts and judges is more carefully scrutinized.

~ ~ ~

Lawyer stories abounded on Richmond's Main Street, reflecting the interaction of unlettered witnesses with intricate court protocol. One lawyer appeared in magistrate's court smelling so strongly of whiskey that the judge called him to his bench for a whispered consultation.

"John Ames," whispered the judge to his old friend, "you smell so God-damned good I could eat you up, meat, bones, and all." The miscreant smiled appreciatively, shook hands, and returned to his seat for the trial to begin.

~ ~ ~

Judge Henry R. Miller, Jr., told me that one witness in his Richmond court testified that he refused to help a defendant because "she act so chauncified." The judge interrupted at that point to ask the meaning of the word.

"Judge, you don' know what chauncified means?" It meant stuck up or arrogant, he was told.

"Thank you," said Judge Miller, and the trial proceeded.

In another court, the judge asked a witness in a shooting case, "Now let me understand, Mrs. Woods. Where were you when you were struck in the fracas?"

"On, no, Judge," the witness responded. "I wasn't struck in

de *fracas.* I was struck in de *navel,* jus a li'l bit *above* de fracas."

Another Main Street courthouse story was of a rural rape case. So crude was the defendant's alleged speech that the judge had the sexual threat written on a piece of paper by the complainant and circulated to the jury, out of respect for the two women in court.

When a male juror passed the exhibit to a woman juror, dozing next to him, she reacted strongly. The exhibit was lettered "I'm goin' to ____ you." Observing the woman's shock, the judge dryly noted, "The court will come to order. The exhibit being circulated to the jury is not to be taken personally. It is alleged by the plaintiff to be the threat made by the defendant."

~ ~ ~

Mr. McDermott, the *Times-Dispatch* city editor, drilled into us reporters the importance of qualification in reporting to avoid possible libel suits. Court reporter Maurice Dean took it to heart when he described a homicide in Jackson Ward. "The dead man's pockets contained approximately $2.67 in cash," Maurice wrote.

~ ~ ~

Richmond's Main Street in the war years was becoming almost as well known for its lawyers as for its sweet-scented tobacco. Virginians from the beginning liked the profession of law, creating the first college law courses in the nation at William and Mary in 1779.

When I worked in Richmond, it had two sizable law firms, one called Hunton Williams Anderson Gay and Moore ("Huntin' and Gruntin'") and the other McGuire Woods Eggleston and Bocock; it is now McGuire Woods Battle and Boothe. The most talked-about of these attorneys was bachelor Henry Watkins Anderson of the Hunton firm, now called Hunton Williams, who had made a fortune as receiver for the Seaboard Airline Railway.

He was called "Colonel" for his service as American Red Cross commissioner in World War I Rumania, where he won the favor—nobody knew how *much* favor—of Queen Marie. Beyond his professional life, Colonel Anderson was admired for his taste—his palatial Franklin Street house, chauffeured limousine (the chauffeur in uniform), and his identification with the nascent Virginia Museum of Fine Arts, where he succeeded Francophile Blythe Branch as chairman. Plain old WASP Richmond was wowed by Col. Anderson's Gallic pizazz.

Newport News *Daily Press*

Lewis Powell, Jr. had a whirlwind career as a Richmond lawyer and civic leader before President Nixon named him to United States Supreme Court.

But the rising star of the Richmond bar was then Lewis F. Powell, Jr., who was to lead in rewriting Richmond's charter and to become chairman of its school board in the rocky years preceding and during racial integration. Powell's father was a rock-ribbed conservative, but the son was a constructive moderate who saw the need for social change. In the forthcoming Virginia struggle over the Byrd-backed "Massive Resistance" to public school integration, Lewis Powell would play a leading role.

I had heard much about Lewis at Washington and Lee,

where he graduated before me in college and then from its law school and from Harvard law school. When President Richard Nixon appointed him to the United States Supreme Court in 1972, it proved a highly successful choice. He was Richmond's first Supreme Court Justice since John Marshall.

Devoted to Richmond and to Virginia, Lewis Powell had turned down an invitation from the famous John W. Davis to join his New York firm after law school. At first he worked with the Richmond firm of Christian, Barton, and Parker before moving to the larger firm and becoming Colonel Anderson's protégé.

Wrote Lewis Powell later of Colonel Anderson (quoted in Anne Hobson Freeman's delightful *The Style of a Law Firm*):

> When he traveled any distance, he used his private railroad car as chairman of Seaboard, and he maintained a suite at the old Ritz-Carlton in New York. I accompanied him to New York on occasion and was fascinated by his status at this European-style hotel. Upon arrival he did not check in. He was recognized by room clerks and bellman alike, maids unpacked his luggage, and when he left the dining room he signed no check and left no gratuities. Responding to my questions about this, he said that signing checks and giving cash gratuities were unnecessary, as everyone knew who he was. At Christmas he would send, from his farm in Dinwiddie County, a large shipment of hams and food products to be distributed to the staff and service people at the Ritz-Carlton.

One of Richmond's eminent attorneys before my day should have been named to the Supreme Court but wasn't.

He was Spencer Roane, who was chief justice of the Virginia Supreme Court when President John Adams in a "midnight appointment," on January 31, 1801, named John Marshall, also of Richmond, to the federal post.

Jefferson, who was about to take office as president, had planned to appoint Roane as chief justice of the United States and was furious with Adams. Roane was a Jeffersonian states' rightist, whose philosophy differed strongly from Marshall's. The history of the United States would have been very different if Roane had been chief justice instead of Marshall.

Roane's Virginia court in Richmond differed bitterly with Marshall's in Washington. Once when the Marshall court overruled Virginia's, Roane and each of Virginia's high court judges took written issue, each writing a rebuttal, but Marshall's court prevailed. Most Virginians profess to be Jeffersonians, but many are closer to the Republican tenets of Marshall.

Richmond's two major law firms since Lewis Powell's day have grown greatly, with offices in other cities and abroad. In 1995 Hunton Williams had 444 attorneys, and McGuire, Woods, Battle and Boothe had 405.

One of Richmond's authors in my newspaper days was Rebecca Yancey Williams, wife of physician John Bell Williams. In 1942 she wrote a hilarious biography of her father, who had been commonwealth's attorney of Lynchburg, called *The Vanishing Virginian*. In it she explained why Virginians are loath to accept "new people" until they've had time–sometimes as much as 50 years–to size them up. Wrote Rebecca:

> Of course Mother's people were every bit as nice as Father's. But Mother's father was from Winchester. While everyone knows Winchester is in Virginia, and is a

charming old town, still my mother's father had not been born in the place where he lived. That offended an English sensibility which still clings to Virginians. I myself do not know how to explain this sensibility unless the general idea is that if a person amounted to anything where he came from he never would have left there. . . .

Author's Collection

Southside Virginia traded in Richmond, whose stores, theaters, and restaurants beckoned. Cotton and tobacco grow heavily below the James.

As a Newport News product living in Richmond, I knew how Rebecca Yancey's mother must have felt. Just grin and bear it.

The personification of the country lawyer was William Munford Tuck, who took office in 1942 as lieutenant-governor, serving under Colgate Darden. He was a Byrd man, but he had a mind and a style of his own. He was a master of the put-down. He once called Senator A. Willis Robertson "as skittery as a fart in a hot skillet."

Jim Latimer, my fellow Capitol Hill reporter, called Tuck "strictly Southside. Very homey in his rustic humor. He had several categories of 'sons of bitches.' The first was a 'common son of a bitch.' Next was 'a spider-legged son of a bitch.' Finally there was a 'common, spider-legged, tip-toeing son of a bitch with oak leaf clusters."' Jim had great respect for the old boy.

Bill Lashley, another former Richmond newspaperman, cherished Tuck's good-natured chastisement of newspaperman Ben Wahrman as a "tiptoeing, feather-footed son of a bitch." It was said with a smile, though, so it didn't hurt. Ben just laughed.

There never was a better talker than Bill Tuck, who presided over the State Senate in my Richmond days. He knew dozens of anecdotes he had used on juries. There was the old man cleaning the shad. When the fish squirmed, the old man admonished, "Hold still, little fish. I ain't gon' do nuthin' but gut ya." Any legislator who tried to eviscerate a bill thereafter was said to be giving it "the shad treatment." Richmond novelist Garrett Epps used it as title for a novel.

Tuck went on to succeed Darden as governor of Virginia after I went in the Navy. When strikers threatened to close the Virginia Electric and Power Company, Tuck didn't hesitate to call out the National Guard to maintain service. It made him a hero across the nation.

~ ~ ~

Richmond Newspapers

Sunshine Sue and her "Barn Dance" performed each weekend at Richmond's WRVA Theater, sometimes attended by her admirer, Governor Bill Tuck.

Mrs. Tuck was a shy woman who often went home from Richmond to Halifax, leaving Big Bill rattling around alone in the Governor's Mansion. On Saturday nights he walked over to the WRVA Theater on Ninth Street to enjoy big brunette Sunshine Sue and her Dixie Hillbillies. Soon Bill and Sue were romantically linked in gossip.

Weighing over 250 pounds but always neatly dressed, Tuck craved company and often begged legislators to stay at the Mansion when his wife was away. He said he was afraid of ghosts. Bourbon was his drink, and Old Guckenheimer, Old Crow, and Old 1889 fueled many of his speeches. Lawmakers did their best wheeling and dealing over drinks at night at their hotels or the Commonwealth Club. Never underestimate the value of a well-timed highball or a funny story.

The Civil War was a favorite theme. Bill Tuck liked to tell of the Alabama hothead who had urged his state to secede in 1861. He disappeared in mortal embarrassment after Lee's surrender, and when he finally came out he was angrily confronted by those whom he had misled. "Yes, I said we could whup them Yankees with cawnstawks," he blurted, "but them damn fool Yankees wouldn't *fight* with cawnstawks."

Most of us newsmen at first judged Tuck a buffoon who would do only what Byrd told him, but we were wrong. Governor Tuck had a mind of his own, and he got laws passed that Virginia needed. His program was applauded by the *Times-Dispatch*, but when editor Virginius Dabney got sick, publisher Jack Wise took over the editorials and lambasted Tuck's program. Tuck never forgave the newspaper for letting him down.

One night Bill was being chauffeured out of the Capitol grounds when he noticed two men embracing on a park bench. "Look at those damned fools, Luther," he fumed to his chauffeur. "Can you imagine making love to a man?" Next day he had the benches moved out of Capitol Square.

I was present when Washington and Lee gave Bill Tuck an honorary degree as an alumnus. The citation began facetiously, "You have soared with the Byrds," which caused Bill to frown disapprovingly. True, he had been elected with the support of the Byrd organization, but he had followed his own judgment once in office. He was a man of principle. He had exceeded all expectations.

Virginia Historical Society

Looking east on Broad Street, trolley tracks separate "right side" from "wrong." On the "wrong" side were saloons, while the right contained department stores and hotels.

14

'The Wrong Side' of Broad

RIDING THE POLICE BEAT nightly with Red McCalley, I made the acquaintance of Richmond's black neighborhood, Jackson Ward. It was a more lawful area than today, now that drugs and guns have boosted Richmond's homicide rate to one of the highest in the nation. Jackson Ward in the 1940s seemed positively peaceful. It was a city in itself, undiscovered by white Richmonders.

Even so, it had its problems—wife beatings, robberies, holdups, drunkenness, murder. Each night we reporters followed the police cars to trouble spots. I discovered the world of Jackson Ward's "numbers" writers, who took bets that rarely paid off, and its weekly collectors of burial insurance money. Bill "Bojangles" Robinson had grown up in Jackson Ward, before he became a headline dancer in New York. So had many jazz musicians, preachers, and scholars.

Trouble was, it was on "the wrong side" of Broad. Whites avoided that side of the avenue—a mind-set surviving from wide-open 19th-century days, when that side of Broad was lined with saloons for an all-male clientele. But by the 1940s the ghetto's "Little Africa" had given way to stores, churches, drugstores and even its own newspaper, the *Afro-American*. Even so, few whites ventured there.

Jackson Ward had a life of its own, apart from white Richmond. Like the black Charleston of "Porgy and Bess," it had its own entertainment, especially after dark. Many of its buildings had originated as graceful 19th-century "Court End" housing, as I learned from Mary Wingfield Scott's *Houses of Old Richmond*, which opened my eyes to Richmond's past.

Richmond Newspapers

Black community life centers in the homes and churches of black Richmond's Jackson Ward, on the north side of Broad Street. Once quiet, the area is now beset with drugs.

After that, I looked at Jackson Ward through different glasses. True, most of it was ill-kempt, but some houses had been crafted by tasteful builders in Classical or Federal style. Some dated back to the 1790s–just after Richmond became Virginia's capital. They had started around Shockoe Valley at the east end of town in the days of tobacco-curing and flour-milling. Some were rowhouses like Baltimore's, each only 25 or 30 feet wide, with an English basement half underground, and with two and a half stories above ground.

The chief charm of Jackson Ward lay in its beautiful wrought iron porches and fences, linking it with romantic Savannah, Charleston, and New Orleans. Mary Wingfield Scott was right: Jackson Ward *was* unique. It is now on the National Register of Historic Places, frequently written about by architects.

Remnants of Richmond's outdoor markets survived at Fifth and Marshall Streets in those days. In the faded market place were dozens of booth-renters who sold produce, flowers, poultry, and meat. Most drove in from the country in early morning, with trucks full of produce. Most of it was fresh and sold at a premium before nightfall. Customers shopped there daily and knew vendors by name.

At Christmas the market was fragrant with cedar trees, wreaths, holly, mistletoe, and running cedar. It was much like the memorable post-Civil War paintings of Richmond by William Ludwell Sheppard in the Valentine Museum. Hanover County produce always seemed to enjoy special favor. "Do those tomatoes come from Hanover?" shoppers would ask.

At the market you could find dressed wild game–squirrel, rabbit, possum, and even muskrat. Chitterlings, tripe, hog maws, "Rocky Mountain oysters" (hog testicles), and other

Newport News *Daily Press*

Dancer Bill "Bojangles" Robinson grew up in Richmond and achieved fame on Broadway. He appeared with Shirley Temple in "The Little Colonel."

rural delicacies were there, too. "Possum mighty good with sweet potatoes," one black vendor told me. Also widely sold were brown eggs laid by "free-ranging" chickens, which country folk prefer to grocery-store white ones.

The effects of racial division were highly visible then, before the courts began to rule that "white only" segregation in stores, buses, trains, hotels, and theaters was unconstitutional. Most of the foot traffic on the north side of Broad was black, while that on the south side was white. The majority of blacks were reluctant to enter Miller and Rhoads or Thalhimers to shop, feeling themselves unwanted.

Gradually, ornate old vaudeville houses like the Colonial and National on "the wrong side" of Broad were taken over as movie houses for blacks, leaving whites to patronize the downtown Loew's, the midtown Byrd, and scattered neighborhood theaters. Broad Street split Richmond into two worlds–black and white.

Jackson Ward was proud of "Bojangles" Robinson, who was

then at the top of his fame on Broadway and in the movies, tap dancing merrily. He starred in pictures with Shirley Temple and Will Rogers. As a boy in Richmond, Bill Robinson had been befriended by no less than cantankerous old Justice John Crutchfield. Robinson loved his native city. A statue of him was later erected at Leigh and Adams Streets, near his childhood home.

Another Jackson Ward luminary was Freeman F. Gosden, who had worked as a boy in the Stephen Putney shoe factory on Broad and developed a genius for mimicry which he exploited as "Amos" of "Amos and Andy" radio fame, then at its peak. Most Richmonders, black and white, tuned in nightly to that program, following Lowell Thomas's 15-minute newscast. Gosden and his "Andy," Charles Gorrell, enjoyed a radio audience of 40,000,000 Americans in those wartime years.

One of the celebrated preachers in Richmond's history was a black, John Jasper, born a slave and the youngest of 24 children. He preached colorful sermons that attracted worshippers of both races to his Sixth Mount Zion Baptist Church, still standing on Duval Street in Jackson Ward. All that was well before my day.

Jasper's specialty was "De Sun Do Move," which he preached over 250 times. Contrary to scientific dogma, Jasper believed, the sun moves around the earth, because the Bible says so. To Jasper and many black Christians, the Bible was "the sum and substance of all knowledge."

By the mid 1940s, as black and white Americans fought overseas, race relations became so delicate that black dialect stories were no longer told on stage. The popularity of "Amos and Andy" waned, and Negro spirituals suddenly seemed to embarrass blacks. Moderates—including the Richmond papers—were urging an end to the Jim Crow laws Virginia had adopted from the Deep South states in 1902, designed to separate the races and to subordinate blacks. But the Byrd organization was unmoved.

I was proud of the newspapers for fighting Jim Crow, even though many of my West End friends derided them.

Richmond Newspapers

Buildings in Richmond's Jackson Ward, where blacks live, go back to colonial times. Here an 18th-century house adjoins a 19th-century church.

~ ~ ~

The South's dependence on black household help was also coming to an end. No longer would white children be reared, as I and my brothers were, by a black matron who was also cook, laundress, and confessor. Blacks by the 1940s could make more money in business downtown.

Ever since Reconstruction, blacks both north and south had worked as domestics in white households. Each morning, the housewives of Jackson Ward would take the trolley to white neighborhoods to work for $1 a day, plus meals and carfare. To this was added hand-me-down clothes and sometimes a small pension in old age.

Despite low pay, "hiring out" had been a life-saver for ex-slaves from Reconstruction, for most white employers were kind and came to regard their black "help" as members of the family. After the war I came to miss the close association with the Julias and Delias and Cornelias who had served my family.

~ ~ ~

Keeping house in pre-air-conditioned years in the South was ritualistic, with the family sitting down three times a day to served meals, a ceremonial Sunday dinner after church, and a ritualistic "grace" or "blessing," uttered by the head of the house at each meal. A few households, like that of the Lewis Williamses—the "Pious Williamses" of Westhampton—even said morning and evening prayers with servants attending, a remnant of Queen Victoria's time.

Few Richmond houses or offices were air-conditioned in the early 1940s, but windows were kept shut and curtains drawn, to be opened only after the sun went down. Most housekeepers replaced winter carpets with straw rugs or left floors bare in summer, covering furniture with white linen

Virginia Gazette

Archibald and Molly McCrea show off their Carter's Grove restoration, carried out while John D. Rockefeller, Jr. was restoring Williamsburg.

slipcovers. Porch-sitting was popular everywhere till air conditioning came along.

Most West End houses had a hand-painted family crest or two hung in the hall, with pastel portraits of the owners' children in the dining room. Many families cherished inherited furniture or portraits, especially if they had been long in the family. Likenesses of Confederate ancestors were common. Upholstered furniture was protected by lace antimacassars, a survival from Victorian years when Macassar oil hair dressing stained upholstery.

Jackson Ward provided labor for white Richmond's gardens, parties, and sewing. The Depression still lingered in the Ward in 1940, when I came there, and many blacks and whites sought work. Unemployed blacks could be hired off the street in Jackson Ward, as Miss Ellen Bagby had hired Sam Robinson when she needed him at Jamestown.

Rationing of food, liquor, and gas was a problem in the war. Many other needs could be met by Miller and Rhoads and Thalhimers, longtime Broad Street rivals, from their basement economy stores up to their high-style women's wear on floors above. Most women thought Thalhimers more youthful, but everybody liked Miller and Rhoads salespeople and its stylish tea room.

Woolworth's on Broad Street next to Miller and Rhoads had two lunch counters–one for blacks and one for whites. Other Broad Street lunch counters encouraged blacks to sit at one end and whites at the other.

Grace Street, paralleling Broad, was the place for specialty shops like Montaldo's and LaVogue. There stood Loew's rococo movie palace, and there stood the Methodists' Cokesbury

Richmond Newspapers

Old-fashioned soul food was dispensed by Richmond's outdoor market, now revived in Shockoe Bottom. The vendor sells meat and produce in winter.

Bookstore, where I was once surprised to find the raunchy best seller, *The Happy Hooker*, on sale. Nearby were other shops, many now moved: E. B. Taylor's china store, the Capri and Occidental restaurants, Foster's and Dementi's photographic studios, Biggs' furniture reproductions, and the Richmond Art Company. Most of these have moved.

The Richmond papers encouraged participation in civic affairs, and many blacks played a role, led by professors at Virginia Union University and by black bankers and lawyers. By the time of World War II, many black lawyers practiced in Richmond. One of the best was Oliver W. Hill, who would later argue in favor of public school integration before the United States Supreme Court and would be the first black elected to Richmond City Council in this century. He recently received an honorary degree from William and Mary.

Mrs. Arthur Caperton, who wrote short stories as Helena Lefroy Caperton, lived on West Avenue and reared a son and five attractive daughters in an upstairs apartment. There she employed a seamstress named Minnie to make her daughters' clothes. One day Minnie called to say her consumptive brother Joe had died and she couldn't come to work. Would Mrs. Caperton have a suit Joe could be buried in?

"I thought of those suits of Ambassador Bingham's that Barry had sent me from Louisville when the Ambassador died," Mrs. Caperton recalled. Her eldest daughter, Mary, had married Barry Bingham, son of Franklin Roosevelt's ambassador to the Court of St. James's, Robert Worth Bingham. "I had the Ambassador's maroon tailcoat and forest green tailcoat, and then there was the cutaway he wore to the Ascot races. I told Minnie, 'Yes, indeed, I've got just the thing for Joe, and you can pick it up right away.'"

Minnie returned to thank Mrs. Caperton after the funeral. "What a beautiful affair," the sewing lady said. "Joe looked so handsome in Mr. Bingham's suit, lying there with his tail coat with gloves and gray top hat on his chest! I had to sit up with the body all night for fear somebody would steal his clothes."

Laughing at her own story, Helena Caperton liked to say, "I couldn't wait to call Barry in Louisville and tell him what had happened to his father's Ascot. He was delighted. 'Father would enjoy that as much as you and I do,'" the publisher told his mother-in-law.

Among Jackson Ward's businesses was Home Beneficial Life Insurance, headquartered at 3901 Broad. Formed many years ago, the company wrote much of its coverage for black subscribers who wanted burial insurance and paid a "route man" for it by the week. The prosperous firm has five district offices in Richmond today, but it started small.

To encourage subscribers when it started, the company sent a representative to the funeral of its first insured to die. Just as

Richmond Newspapers

Markets have flourished in Richmond since John Marshall's day. Farmers and produce buyers sell wares "straight from the country."

the funeral ended, the insurance agent stepped up to the widow and, in sight of mourners, counted out a hundred crisp new bills for all to see. It was an inspired promotion. The company lived happily ever after.

Before Mary Wingfield Scott began her campaign to save old Richmond, many buildings were torn down to make way for "progress." Fortunately, Miss Scott was rich, so she bought and saved several buildings, including Linden Row's 19th-century facade on Franklin Street, now a hotel. She also compiled two books of the history and architecture of the city's buildings, alerting posterity to continue the work.

All this helped create a huge demand for old building materials, like wrought-iron railings, that are no longer easily available to home-builders. Today several firms make a business of buying up such materials from demolitions. One is Caravati's Salvage Yard, which occupies several acres on Second Street, still doing a lively business. It looks like a junkyard but is crammed with architectural goodies.

One buyer of Caravati's wares was Mrs. Archibald McCrea, who in my Richmond days restored Carter's Grove plantation near Williamsburg. One day in the 1940s when Mollie McCrea was driving through Richmond, she saw workmen removing worn cobblestones from a street close to the James. She made her chauffeur stop while she got out and learned that Caravati's had bought the cobblestones. Soon they were delivered to her at Carter's Grove, where they are part of the driveway today.

"I'm the Vandal of Virginia," Mrs. McCrea boasted in President John Stewart Bryan's guest book at the College of William and Mary. She had the charm–and money–to get away with it.

~ ~ ~

Artist Margaret Dashiell caught a glimpse of old Richmond in a cartoon she showed me. It showed two black nurses in starched white, tending to several little white boys in Monroe Park. "Mind yo' manners, chile," one nurse barks to her young charge. "Manners git you whar money won't."

Asked what her mistress did all day, another housemaid told me, "Miss Helen jes' sets and po's tea." When Miss Helen married for the first time, in her 60s, to a worldly widower, a friend asked her housemaid if she thought Miss Helen was up to it. "Oh, yes ma'am," the maid said, "but she gonna have to stretch ev'vy nerve." She was unconsciously quoting the words of Philip Doddridge, who in 1775 wrote the popular hymn, "Awake My Soul, Stretch Every Nerve."

And coming out of church one Sunday, one black matron was overheard rebutting another, "I don't care what you say. Yo mouf ain' no prayer book."

An elderly woman told me in Richmond–and I've lived to know it's true–"Whatever you is when you's young, you just gits more so when you's old." She complained that her husband was getting "high-rumpted."

In similar vein, Joe Bryan III wrote of a Gloucester black woman's explanation of why an inbred boy was weak-witted. Said she, astutely, "He too close kin to hissef."

When John Stewart Bryan attended the reopening of Kenmore, the Lewis plantation at Fredericksburg, he was greeted by an elderly black butler, who was trying to control rambunctious guests awaiting entry. "Nice folks don't shove," the butler observed, reprovingly. Mr. Bryan often recalled the admonition.

One Richmond cook asked her mistress to explain to her the virgin birth of Christ. "I knows the story," the cook said, "but what was the adVAN-tage of it?"

I enjoyed the talk of Jackson Ward and the chastisements I heard there. "You so dumb," one speaker assailed another, "you don' know whether Jesus Christ was crucified or killed in the Battle of Bull Run." Other victims were derided as "trundle-bed trash" or as "nuthin' but breath and britches." Familiar too were such similes as "poor as Job's turkey hen" and "wild as a billygoat."

My Richmond friend, Maria Sheerin, liked to say she spoke only two languages, white and colored. You needed them then in Richmond.

One night Mr. McDermott, the *Times-Dispatch* city editor, sent me to a house in Jackson Ward to get a photograph of a woman killed on Broad Street that day, when she leaped from a car in motion. She had been forced into the car by a pistol-toting wife who accused her of husband-stealing and was taking her to the police. The accused promptly jumped out of the moving car, broke her neck, and died. The *Times-Dispatch* wanted me to obtain her picture for the paper.

When I nervously approached the front door to ask for the woman's photograph, I could hear the family sobbing. No, indeed, they wouldn't provide any photograph, one of the family told me at the door, and I couldn't blame them. I felt sick in my stomach and went back to Mr. McDermott empty-handed.

In a rundown service station near the Medical College of Virginia, I met a self-taught local historian named Slim Speight. He did a thriving business running his station and parking lot, but he preferred finding cheap antiques for grateful friends. Richmond had a lot of amateur antiquarians, who liked to talk history and to dabble in genealogy as well as in old books, maps, prints, and furniture. Slim was one. He had never been to college, but he had a world of knowledge.

When I first visited Slim's service station, my eye fell on his storeroom of antiquities. "If you see anything you like, I'll be glad to make you a price," he said. He sold me five 19th-century Webster chairs for $7 apiece and two handsome 18th-century pine bedside candle stands for $10 apiece. Later, when I was married, I bought a lot of Slim's pickings and enjoy them with my family today.

15

Richmond's Pecking Order

ONE MONDAY in my last month in Richmond, the city editor sent me to the Woman's Club to cover a talk by John Mason Brown, New York drama critic and messiah of the lecture circuit. This wasn't your ordinary woman's club, which is big on good works; instead, the chief aim of Richmond's old and exclusive Richmond Woman's Club was to hear top speakers. The 1500 members are the upper crust of WASP Richmond. A lot of them have their own trust funds.

Ladies wore hats in those days, and they were a sight to see. Many were the fancy creations of Sarah Sue Sherrill, Miller and Rhoads' stylish milliner, and reminded me of the galleons of the Spanish Armada, in full sail. I called them DAR hats.

I entered the handsome old club house, built on Franklin Street as the Bolling Haxall residence, to find myself one of a half-dozen males among several hundred ladies. I recognized many of the city's dowagers, all dying to hear the latest from the world of Manhattan. They all called the speaker "John Mason" from his prior visits.

Soon we were laughing at his sophisticated wit, his elegant word play, and his Yale erudition. Richmond prefers its intel-

Virginia Historical Society

Talk about the good old days! Left to right are Mrs. E. Randolph Williams, Miss Adele Clarke, Lady Astor, and Miss Ellen Bagby, once school-girls together.

lectuality in Ivy League accents, bow-tied, and offhandedly humorous. And no bad words!

Every Monday afternoon except in summer Richmond ladies gathered to hear such a lecture, to take tea with the speaker, and then to go home to titillate their husbands with the latest excesses from up north. In a way the Woman's Club was the distaff version of the Commonwealth Club, though it was much more purposeful. It vied for top billing in Bob Munford's "old Richmond" obituaries, along with the Country Club, the Colonial Dames, the Society of the Cincinnati, and the James River and Tuckahoe Garden Clubs.

One of Virginia's most admired dowagers was Gay Montague Moore, daughter of long-ago Governor Andrew Jackson Montague and widow of Colonel Charles Beattie Moore. She divided her life between Alexandria and Gloucester, where she lived in old age at historic Toddsbury. Christening a ship in Newport News one day, the gutsy old lady fell into conversation with Admiral Hyman Rickover, who teasingly asked, "Mrs. Moore, have you ever committed adultery?" She replied sweetly, "Not yet, Admiral. Not yet."

Once she entertained at a party where one guest absentmindedly plucked what looked like hors d'oeuvres from a bowl on her dining room table. Finally she interrupted: "Mr. McMurran, you're eating my potpourri!"

More than any other city I know, Richmond had a pecking order. Most Woman's Club members were WASPs, once dominated by members from "old Richmond" but now succumbing to Mrs. Catterall's go-getter Junior Leaguers. It was all grounded, I decided, in Richmond's private prep schools, which enroll alumni children at conception and retain them, more or less isolated from the opposite sex, until college. ("I've just enrolled my fetus in Collegiate," one woman told

Authors Collection

The Bolling Haxall house, built from flour mill riches in 1858, houses Richmond's exclusive Woman's Club, which brings speakers to discuss social and artistic subjects.

me.) Popular summer camps like Camp Virginia (boys) and Camp Merriewood Harrison (girls) also shared in this intensive youthful bonding.

As if that weren't enough, graduates of St. Somebody's in Richmond like to go off to a few popular nearby colleges. Top choices of males were the University of Virginia, Hampden-Sydney, VMI, and a few Northern schools. The girls now favor the now-coeducational University, and other coed campuses, though in my day, when the University was all male, they thronged to Hollins and Sweet Briar, where mommy had gone.

After college graduation and a few years' work in Richmond or some other "in" city, Richmonders marry other Richmonders and settle down in the Fan or West End. To the city's credit, a large percentage of its natives elect to stay in their hometown, though this gets a bit incestuous after several generations. Occasionally, cousin marries cousin, which gives more work to psychiatrists.

I was struck by the similarity of Richmond's dynastic pattern and that of New York's Jewish clans which Steve Birmingham described in his account of New York's wealthy Jewish bankers, *Our Crowd*. Tribal ambition leads both Gentile and Jew to push his young to burnish the family image. That means succeeding big in life and playing a conspicuous role in civic and social affairs.

The values exalted by these dynasty-builders are those so-called "middle-class" virtues enshrined by WASPs since the days of King Arthur: loyalty, honesty, patriotism, spirituality, courage, gratitude, generosity. Richmonders justify sending their offspring to expensive church preparatory schools for the spirituality and character building they provide.

Before the two World Wars, Virginia was an even more

inbred society than today. In Victorian days only two or three percent of Virginia residents had been born outside the State. However, two wartime waves of soldiers and sailors have left many newcomers. As the genealogists put it, we have enlarged our gene pool, to Mrs. Catterall's regret.

~ ~ ~

An insight into early Virginia's parental attitudes was provided by editor Wendell Garrett in the magazine *Antiques* in 1992. He wrote:

> In the South, the aristocracy of birth and manners more nearly approached its counterpart in England than in anything else to be found in America. There, to a degree unknown in the North, the Virginia patrician William Fitzhugh [1651–1701] spoke for his class in avowing that his children had "better be never born than illbred." The southern gentry reinforced its position by matrimonial alliances, and the rare instances of the "gentle folk" marrying beneath their station scandalized friends and kinsmen.
>
> To William Byrd II [1674–1744] it was nothing short of a "tragic Story" when a wellborn Virginia girl in 1732 played "so senceless a Prank" as to marry her uncle's overseer, "a dirty Plebeian." The owners of the great plantations, resting on a vital distinction between slave labor and gentlemanly leisure, educated their sons abroad, made annual migrations to summer watering places, and prided themselves on keeping abreast of the modish fashions of London society. . . .
>
> As befitted their social position, this colonial gentry occupied the seats of power in provincial politics, safeguarding their privileges by restricting the right to vote

only to white adult males who possessed a stated amount of property and who, in most provinces, had to subscribe to certain religious tenets.

Some WASPs still would "better be never born than ill-bred," as William Fitzhugh thought in the reign of the Stuarts.

Along with its Anglo-Saxon pioneers, Richmond also acquired a few Jewish newcomers whose talents contributed to the city's life. They were mostly Sephardics from Spain and Portugal, who came soon after the American Revolution, before the 19th-century Jewish influx from Central Europe. After the Civil War came Ashkenazi Jews from Germany, Poland, and Russia, many through the ports of Baltimore and Norfolk. A network of Richmond Jews helped newcomers up the ladder.

Among the colonial Richmond Jews were the Myerses, Mordecais, Oppenhimers, and Cardozos, whose descendants were Christianized and are absorbed as Gentiles. When naturalist John James Audubon came to Richmond in 1840 to obtain subscribers for his *The Birds of America* folio, he enlisted 29 well-to-do gentlemen, including four Jewish subscribers: Dr. Frederick Marx, and three members of the Myers family of Richmond and Norfolk: G. A. Myers, Dr. Henry Myers, and William R. Myers.

By the time of World War II, Richmond's Jewish population was extensive and influential. Some of these were Millhiser, Schwarzchild, Thalhimer, Binswanger, Bendheim, Straus, Hutzler, Klaus, and Marcuse. Many resided in fine houses on upper Monument Avenue. However, there were then no Jewish members of the Commonwealth or Country Club of Virginia. They came later, well after World War II.

~ ~ ~

Since its founding by "the Black Swan of Westover" on the shores of the James, Richmond has moved westward. After the Civil War tobacconist Lewis Ginter developed Ginter Park north of the rail lines through town. The generous Ginter gave land there for the Presbyterians' Union Theological

Virginia Historical Society

An 1893 photo of a Richmond private school–perhaps Miss Jennie Ellett's, the precursor of St. Catherine's. From such starts grew the city's church-based prep schools.

Seminary as well as their School of Christian Education. These have made Richmond's northside somewhat Presbyterian, built along old Brook Road and wide thoroughfares like Chamberlayne, Laburnum, and Confederate avenues.

Later, the growth of the Country Club of Virginia and of the campus of the University of Richmond in Westhampton helped redirect Richmond back westward along the James. It was fortunate, for the river offered the city's best views. Today the city steadily moves north towards Goochland County, with the river as its axis.

Richmond neighborhoods in World War II had a pecking order. At the top was Westhampton along the James, from Windsor Farms to Goochland. Less stylish was the area from the Boulevard to Windsor Farms. The midtown, from Monroe Park westward to the Boulevard, was full of newlyweds, now known as yuppies. Richmond calls that the Fan District, radiating out from Monroe Park. Left far behind at the unstylish east end is old Church Hill, where houses in the 1700s centered around Henrico Parish Church, now St. John's, where Patrick Henry made that speech.

Few people have more greatly influenced Richmond than the founders of its church schools. Their motive was to provide a Christian theology, which public schools are not permitted to emphasize. Two remembered founders were W. Gordon McCabe, who moved his boys' school from Petersburg to Richmond after the Civil War and conducted it for six years before retiring. McCabe taught, among many others, Churchill Chamberlayne, who in 1911 opened his own school and in 1920 became headmaster of St. Christopher's, when it was bought from him by the Episcopal Diocese of Virginia and enlarged.

Another remembered schoolmaster was John Peyton McGuire II, who founded McGuire's University School in 1865, kept going by his namesake son until 1942. Many living Richmonders were educated by John Peyton McGuire III, called "Boss." The school is sadly mourned by its surviving alumni, called "McGuire's Boys," who meet annually.

Revered at Collegiate, a Presbyterian school, is the memory of headmistress Mrs. William Flippen, who served before the girls' and boys' schools were merged. Rivalry between Collegiate and its Episcopal counterparts is genteel but strong. Each tries to place its graduates in the best possible colleges.

The best remembered Richmond school founder was Virginia Randolph Ellett, known as "Miss Jennie," who started her girls' school in 1890 and ran it until it became a country day school in Westhampton in 1917. There it was bought by the Episcopal Diocese of Virginia as a counterpart to St. Christopher's and christened St. Catherine's. Apologizing for Miss Jennie's Waspish emphasis on status, one admiring pupil, Mrs. Natalie Blanton, has acknowledged Miss Jennie's "recognition of the power of wealth and prestige." She especially hoped her graduates would live graciously, even if they were poor.

~ ~ ~

Miss Jennie Ellett was an Anglophile who attended Oxford and aped the practices of English schools in her own teaching at St. Catherine's. Education for females then ran to religion and aesthetics, overlooking vocational subjects. Her curriculum centered on history, English, and the Bible. Miss Jennie wanted her girls to develop their minds to their best, and pushed them toward good colleges, some in the North. She sent her senior class compositions to be evaluated by a professor of English at Harvard.

A well remembered teacher at Miss Jennie's was Miss Lulie Blair, who led each year's fifth grade girls through their own Olympic games and put her sixth graders through a Roman wedding and a production of Shakespeare, mercifully abbreviated. In "Julius Caesar" one year, Miss Lulie chose little Mamie Taymes Patterson to portray a statue of Pompey, her body dusted with flour to look like marble.

Alas, poor Mamie Taymes got a speck in her eye, and the tears that ran down her face ruined the illusion. Even worse, she had to stand stock still while two of her classmates in turn declaimed Anthony's speech:

> Friends, Romans, countrymen, lend me your ears;
> I come to bury Caesar, not to praise him.
> The evil that men do lives after them.
> The good is oft interred with their bones.

The speech had to be repeated by a second Anthony because Miss Lulie wanted as many students as possible to benefit from learning it. Poor Mamie Taymes Patterson!

One of Miss Jennie's friends was "Miss" Bessie Hobson–Mrs. Saunders Hobson–who lived well into her 90s in a mansion on Monument Avenue. One morning Mrs. Hobson's maid couldn't open her mistress' bedroom door, so she shouted though the crack, "Miss Bessie, where is you?"

"I'm under the ceiling," came the calm reply. "It fell in on me. Call the hospital emergency."

Alas, the plaster ceiling in Mrs. Hobson's bedroom had fallen during the night, imprisoning the 92-year-old lady beneath her bedclothes. When the firemen couldn't open her bedroom door, they put a ladder to her second-floor window, extricated her, and carried her down the ladder to Stuart Circle Hospital. She was unhurt and rushed home to reassure her maid. Miss Bessie enjoyed all of it.

~ ~ ~

The women's page of the *News Leader* was brightened one December day by a photograph of a Richmond debutante in riding clothes, clearing a hurdle on a dappled-gray hunter. The caption read, "Coming Home From School" and explained that the debutante, who went to Sweet Briar, would spend the holidays with her parents on Cary Street Road.

I always suspected that some reader passed that on to Peter Arno, the *New Yorker* cartoonist, who in that magazine later penned a view of a starchy tycoon, gazing through his dining room window at a young equestrian clearing the garden wall. He remarked to his wife, "Here's Deborah, home from school."

~ ~ ~

Richmond dowagers were so outspoken that they were regarded as characters. One was Mrs. E. Randolph Williams, called "Aunt Maude" by her endless Williams kin–a lady who had iron opinions on all subjects. The Frederic Scott family was the most outspoken of all Richmond WASP clans, perhaps because it was so sure of itself. (Money helped.) Beside daughter Elisabeth, who married John (Jack) Bocock, there was Mary Ross ("Rossie") Scott Reed, who mercifully distributed No-Doz tablets to hearers before she made a Garden Club speech on water conservation.

Like Lady Astor and Ellen Bagby, these ex-schoolmates knew each other well enough to be brutally frank. Their nicknames suggest that: Piggy, Boxie, Dumpy, Ducky, Big Eda, and

Phronie. Those who have grown up together will always be young together.

And Richmonders loved clubs. Dr. Freeman had a weekly current-events club at the Commonwealth that attracted top businessmen, while his daughter, Mary Tyler Cheek, conducted a weekly Bible class for West End ladies. The chauffeured limousines that brought the postulants looked more like a gathering of the Fortune 500 than a Bible class.

The University of Virginia holds a special place in Richmond's cosmos. Despite their Republicanism, well-to-do Richmonders genuflect at the mere mention of "Mistuh Jefferson," as UVA grads call him. To many Richmonders, Charlottesville is the western end of civilization. Long lines of station wagons throng Three Chopt Road westward for UVA football games, Easter, and graduation. Before Interstate 64 was built, they all stopped faithfully at a churchyard at Zion Crossroads to picnic and pass the Mason jars of juleps before the kickoff.

Returning to Richmond one autumn Saturday, Mr. and Mrs. Walter Robertson (he was later under secretary of state under Eisenhower) stopped at a Zion Crossroads service station, she driving and he snoozing in the back seat. While she went inside to pay for the gas, Walter Robertson went to the restroom. His wife resumed the drive without bothering to check the back seat to see if Walter were still there. It all made for a strenuous afternoon.

One of Richmond's internists was courtly Douglas Vanderhoof, who was playing golf one day when his partner, the aged

Beirne Blair, collapsed. Dr. Vanderhoof worked over his friend but could not revive him. Sadly he phoned Blair's brother to break the news:

"I say, Lewis: Douglas Vanderhoof speaking. I have some bad news . . . Beirne fell out unconscious on the golf course here at the club." Then pausing thoughtfully to let that sink in, he plunged on: "I'm afraid he has a very weak pulse . . . . . Indeed, he has no pulse at all."

~ ~ ~

Small as it was, Richmond in the nineties had its own printed social register, like those of New York, Boston, and Philadelphia. It listed residence, family, college or university, and the club memberships of each registrant. Most clubs were called German or dance societies, which met on specified nights. The Richmond of Chiswell Dabney Langhorne's day was a social hive.

~ ~ ~

In the early 1940s I had a great interest in rare books, Civil War autographs, and antique furniture, even though I had no immediate prospect of marriage. Richmond had many antique shops, some pricey like Mr. Navis's on Main Street, but others less fancy, usually on "the wrong side" of Broad. They were where you found bargains. I enjoyed browsing through them on my days off.

One dealer was Mrs. Carrie Duke, widow of the Reverend Frank Duke, who lived on Franklin Street and sold antiques from her collection. I came to know her through Frank and Lilian Eleazer, who lived in her carriage house, furnished with her for-sale antiques. Mrs. Duke was a friend of Ellen Glasgow's, and helped John Stewart Bryan furnish the President's House at William and Mary. The Eleazers frequently had furnishings sold out from under them by Carrie Duke, but they didn't seem to mind.

An autograph and rare book shop in Linden Row had papers written by Lee and Jackson. Mary Clark Roane's Old Collector's Book Shop also offered a hoard of Virginia histories and biographies, sometimes with bookplates of past owners. The past was everywhere.

I spent a lot of my pay buying books by Richmond authors —Freeman, Dabney, Glasgow, and Cabell, but they've meant a lot to me ever since.

~ ~ ~

A friend from Smithfield brought me a picturesque advertisement he had found as backing behind a picture in an old frame, and it proved to be a prize. It turned out to be an ad of my great grand uncle's contracting (then called "undertaking") and furniture business in Smithfield, printed in Norfolk in April 1859. It read:

William Rouse
Cabinet
Manufacturer
Smithfield, Va.
Solicits the patronage of the
citizens of Smithfield and surrounding country, and pledges
himself to use every exertion to give satisfaction. All kinds of
FURNITURE REPAIRED
in the neatest manner and warranted.
Having a first-rate HEARSE, I am prepared to attend to the
UNDERTAKING BUSINESS
in all of its branches, and all orders thankfully received
and promptly attended to
Wm. Rouse

That whetted my appetite for antique-hunting, but I never found anything else equally personal.

~ ~ ~

After the last volume of Dr. Freeman's *R. E. Lee* appeared, I asked Dr. Freeman if he would give the handwritten manuscript to Washington and Lee. He had already given most chapters away to stimulate war-bond buyers, but he gave me four chapters of Lee's last years, as president of the college in Lexington. I was glad to pass them on to my alma mater.

~ ~ ~

Virginia WASPs are big on bloodlines. In the Library of Virginia and the Virginia Historical Society, I encountered genealogists collecting data for clients. People wanted to research their "line" to join one of the patriotic societies. Because 18th-century Virginia was so large, it sent many pioneers to the South and West, whose descendants now come back for their genealogy.

The appeal of bloodlines was summed up by Oliver Wendell Holmes, 19th-century spokesman for New England Waspdom:

> What is called my character, or nature, is made up of infinite particles of inherited tendencies from my ancestors—those whose blood runs in my veins. A little seed of laziness comes from this grandfather, and of prodigality from that other one. One of them may have been a moody person and a pessimist; while another was of jovial nature who always saw the sunny side of every event. One may have had a great satisfactory life as a philosopher; while another ambitious one never was contented with actual conditions what ever they were. Some remote grandmother, perhaps, has stamped me with a fear of dogs

> and a love of horses. There may be in me a bit of outlawry from some pirate forefather and a dash of piety from one to another who was a saint. . . .
>
> My so-called peculiarities: my ways and my mannerisms, I borrowed from all, without any exception. So everything in me passes on through my children. I am sewn between ancestry and posterity. I am a drop of water in the flowing river of time, a molecule in a mountain; a cell in a great family tree.
>
> As we enter life we find all these fears and fancies; likes and dislikes, dispositions and temperament already made in the human beehive, and crawl into them; so that they become a part of our true fibre; part of our personal texture; part of our frame of mind and body.
>
> This is our birthmark; this is our heritage.

It was a WASP sentiment. Dr. Holmes should have lived in Richmond.

Author's Collection

The Commonwealth Club on Franklin Street is a bastion of privileged WASPs. There Robert E. Lee's birthday is celebrated annually amid reminders of the Confederacy.

16

In the Bowels of the Commonwealth

IT IS THE NIGHT of January 19, and at the Commonwealth Club on Franklin Street the tables are laid with silver, candles, and flowers, awaiting the arrival of the full membership. It is Robert E. Lee's birthday, and high rollers from all over Virginia are drifting in to celebrate. It's a high holiday on the WASP calendar.

If he feels up to it, old Rush will deliver Lee's farewell to his troops.

Founded in 1890, the Commonwealth Club merged in 1937 with the older and more scholarly Westmoreland Club, which had long stood on the corner of Sixth and Grace Streets, across from the later Loew's Theater. The merged club, referred to now simply as "the club" or "the Commonwealth," was a bastion of males, though verboten for blacks,

Jews, women, and anti-Byrd politicians. (That changed after World War II.)

I discovered the Commonwealth when I had to write news accounts for the paper about banquets there of the Society of Colonial Wars or of the Sons of the Revolution. Later I became a member. In those days it was to Virginia conservatives what the Alamo was to Sam Houston. Today it is trying to adjust to life in a more egalitarian era. No longer is it regarded by nonmembers as the epitome of WASP exclusivity, though a lot of elitism remains. It now has a few Jewish and black members, though no women.

However much it tries to avoid publicity, the Commonwealth epitomizes the unostentatious good living that Virginians enjoy. The high-pitched Victorian clubhouse has been expanded to accommodate a far-flung membership made up of tycoons, CEOs, politicians, businessmen, and a few sports. Even so, some of the Confederate flavor of the Westmoreland Club back in 1877 persists. The Westmoreland's bar was where aging Confederates traded memories and raised glasses to "our great captain," Marse Robert. That survives in the Commonwealth Club.

The Confederate memory is kept alive by portraits of Lee and his lieutenants and by 1860s genre scenes, painted from life by Richmond's William Ludwell Sheppard and Fredericksburg's John A. Elder. Its original entrance, library, and underground game rooms, panelled in golden oak, are restricted to males, but a "new" side entrance admits ladies to dining and ballroom.

In the basement game rooms—strictly male—are almost continuous rounds of bridge, poker, and gin rummy. By a gentleman's agreement, gambling debts are settled by 9 A.M. following the evening's combat.

~ ~ ~

I first learned about the Westmoreland Club when I researched the career of an eccentric Confederate surgeon, Dr. Bennett W. Green, who frequented the club in the 1880s. That was after he returned from a self-imposed post-Appomattox exile in Brazil and began to compile his A *Word-Book of Virginia Folk-Speech*, published by William Ellis Jones in Richmond in 1899. Green spent many hours in the Westmoreland Club's library. There he knew Colonel William Gordon McCabe, CSA, president of the Virginia Historical Society, who wrote in his 1914 eulogy of Dr. Green:

> He was, in truth, what was called in Virginia fifty years ago "a character"—alas! in these days of telephones and aeroplanes, there are no longer any "characters" left—just "the dead level of mediocrity," as Tocqueville says. He was full of the most delightful prejudices and not a few eccentricities, which made him irresistibly attractive to his intimates.
>
> What was regarded here in Richmond as one of these marked eccentricities (although some may think it deserves a nobler name) was his custom, every day of the year, and year after year, no matter what the weather rain, sleet, or torrid sun—to walk punctually at 4 o'clock P.M. to the Lee Monument, gravely uncover and salute the "presentment" in bronze of our great captain, and then walk back, with sedate step, to his rooms or to his corner of the Westmoreland Club.

Whenever I went to the Commonwealth, I sensed the heroism of those Reconstruction years, when Virginia slowly pulled itself up to become a leader of the New South. But it would never apologize for its Confederate years. The rebel spirit of Bennett Green, CSA, still lives.

When the General Assembly of Virginia met each January, the Commonwealth Club welcomed members who were legislators and lobbyists for a period of about six weeks. It was the

Virginia Historical Society

In the World War II era, Richmond ladies dressed up to go downtown shopping. Today few shop downtown and few dress up.

ideal place for movers and shakers to operate and avoid the eyes of press. At night, the gaming rooms resounded with politics, accompanied by a descant of card talk at the nearby green baize tables. Governors and senators were anointed in its hideaways. Fortunes and political glory have been achieved here.

Richmonders in the 1940s went in for formality at many functions in their clubs and at the Lyric Theater and Mosque Auditorium. Big concerts of the Civic Musical Association drew black tied men and befrocked women, seated in the Mosque's orchestra and Diamond Horseshoe. White tie was the unspoken rule when the Richmond German gathered in the Commonwealth Club ballroom. When one Abingdon guest showed up in a dinner jacket, he precipitated one of the German's worst crises.

And when my fellow reporter, Whitton Morse, was sent to the Commonwealth Club one night to cover an address to the Society of the Cincinnati, nobody told him it was black tie. Whit was surprised when the Cincinnati refused to admit him, even to sit by the door and take notes. His dilemma finally reached the ear of *Times-Dispatch* publisher, John Stewart Bryan. After Mr. Bryan called the club, Whit was quickly admitted.

Those were the days when ladies wore hats and gloves and men wore vests and garters. At St. Paul's Church, a few elderly geezers even attended Christmas and Easter services until World War II in cutaway and top hat. No longer.

Wild game was a specialty of the Commonwealth, and Maryland terrapin stew remains a fixture each January 19 at Lee's birthday dinner, though terrapins are scarce. During shooting season, members bring their quarry to the club's kitchens to be picked and dressed.

The most popular dish on the Commonwealth menu was corncakes with braised oysters, Smithfield ham, and melted butter. This high cholesterol classic was originated by William Rush, who retired from the club in 1945 after many years as maitre d'. It's still on the menu.

Anecdotes of Commonwealth Club life enliven Richmond lore, but efforts to collect and print them have defied such intrepid members as Dr. Charles Caravati. Some of its stories are too raunchy, others too personal, and others too ephemeral. But if the club's members would talk, Richmond would tremble.

And the club has had memorable wits. In his *Richmond, The Story of a City*, Virginius Dabney recalls such expansive bon vivants as J. St. George Bryan, Charles Cotesworth Pinckney, Egbert G. Leigh, Jr., Dr. W. T. Oppenhimer, and John T. "Jake" Anderson. To this list more recently one might add Dr. Thomas Murrell, Sr., and Robert V. Hatcher, Sr. I can see Bob Hatcher now, regaling his table with his good ol' boy stories.

After Dr. Murrell served as club president, he provided in his will that all drinks should be free on the afternoon of his funeral. He preferred this, he said, to having his portrait painted for the club and then never looked at.

A member recalled, "I've never seen so many people crowd into the club as they did for those free drinks. Everybody who belonged showed up to drink to Dr. Murrell."

When Robert V. Hatcher, Sr., was president, he had the unpleasant task of confronting an unidentified stranger dining alone in the club. The interloper turned out to be the Beverly Hills restaurateur, Mike Romanoff, a Brooklyn native who passed himself off as a Russian nobleman. He owned the famous Romanoff's restaurant in Hollywood.

Hatcher politely told Romanoff the club had no reciprocal privileges and asked him not to return after finishing his meal. Years later in Los Angeles, a friend took Bob Hatcher to lunch at Romanoff's restaurant. When Mike Romanoff greeted the two visitors, Hatcher was introduced as from Richmond. "That sunabitch recognized me, I'm sure," the Richmonder recalled, "but he never said a word."

Virginia Historical Society

Richmond celebrated Japan's surrender on September 2, 1945. A News Leader extra proclaimed "JAPS QUIT. WAR IN PACIFIC OVER."

The Commonwealth wasn't just for drinking and card-playing. It had a library to keep its members informed, though not used much, except for The *Wall Street Journal* and *Times-Dispatch*. When the present clubhouse was built, it looked dark and masculine, with heavy wood paneling, but decorators have brightened it. Still, stained oak woodwork and green library lamps give it a Victorian dignity.

The staff too has changed, and young men and women—many of them students at Virginia Commonwealth University—took over as waiters in place of the onetime corps of black servitors. In the new era, I heard one of the pretty blonde bartenders call a waiter to the bar and ask, "Hey, Joe, how do you make a Virgin Mary?"

~ ~ ~

In spite of its politician members, many Commonwealth Club habitues had little use for public servants. A story in the club basement was of the Southside truck driver arrested for speeding near the North Carolina line.

"Haven't you got a governor on that truck?" asked the state trooper who arrested him.

"No suh, boss," said the driver. "Dat ain't no governor you smell. Dat's cow manure." Governor Tom Stanley didn't like that story.

~ ~ ~

Like most rich men, Commonwealth Club members generally deplored Franklin Roosevelt as a traitor to his class. Most were adherents of Harry Byrd and, like him, anxious to keep government small. They were "Byrd Democrats" as opposed to "New Deal Democrats." They liked male prep schools and colleges, wives who stayed home and reared children, summers at the Rivah, well-trained hunting dogs, and movies about rich people. They were WASPs.

They mourned the passing of McGuire's University School, the disappearance of alligators from the Jefferson Hotel lobby, the decline of unlimited duck-shooting, the revocation of the poll tax, and the repeal of Sunday blue laws. They didn't like women in public life or the revision of the Book of Common Prayer. And they hated anti-tobacco laws.

They also missed many casualties of the industrial age: house servants, Confederate idolatry of Lee and Jackson, and river steamers that knit together the tidewater. Life that had once been deliberate and intimate had become fast and furious. A city that had once been small and paternalistic was becoming big, bureaucratic and impersonal. Virginia was getting to be like ordinary states. I could sympathize with some of that.

I was having such a lark in Richmond that I put off leaving as long as I could.

But in 1942, not long after the attack on Pearl Harbor, I revisited the Naval Officer Procurement Office on Lombardy Street and looked up my old W&L professor, Lawrence Watkin. He recommended that I be commissioned as an Air Combat Intelligence officer, which meant I would brief and debrief Navy flyers. But I held out—wrongly, I realized later—for a communications billet. (It turned out to be boring.)

My orders came that summer, sending me to Harvard for a month's indoctrination and four months' communication training. I reported to Harvard yard on September 1, 1942. Goodbye, Richmond.

I spent my last weeks sadly preparing to leave Richmond, a paradoxical city that I had somehow learned to love. But as a 27-year-old male, I was beginning to feel conspicuous in civies. A doctor friend in New York, medically exempt, was accosted about that time by a ferocious woman who demanded "Why aren't you in service, young man?" "Syphilis," he barked back. Fortunately, people in Virginia weren't like that.

On Broad Street one day I encountered sweet old Mrs. Edward Maria Wingfield, whose promising young son John was a new Navy flyer. "How's John?" I asked. That dear lady burst into tears. Hadn't I seen the paper? Young, handsome John had died in a crash.

~ ~ ~

The *Times-Dispatch* staff was changing rapidly, too, as we reporters went off to war. In those last weeks I was often invited to friends' apartments after work to drink and reminisce and speculate. I spent evenings in the company of the Latimers, the Eleazers, and the McNairs. At the Country Club on Saturday nights, we departing ninety-day-wonders wanted to throw caution to the winds and raise cain, but stately old Richmond constrained us. I can still hear the band playing "The Jersey Bounce."

When I told Mr. McDermott goodbye, he was kind. "For a college kid, you did pretty well," he said with a twinkle.

~ ~ ~

I spent most of the next three years on a Navy attack transport, roaming the world. As communications officer of the USS *James O'Hara,* I took part in landings at Sicily, Salerno, and Saipan. In my last year in service, I was on the staff of Admiral Nimitz, commander in chief of the Pacific fleet, in Pearl Harbor and Guam. I was discharged in 1946, a few months after Japan surrendered.

The Richmond I came home to was very different from the one I had left. Everything I enjoyed had increased in price, from Hershey bars to the *New York Times.* But clearly a greater fairness was now evident toward blacks, who had put their lives on the line for Uncle Sam in that terrible war as willingly as the rest of us. I thought back to a verse by Robert Louis Stevenson my mother had taught to me when I was a child:

> Little Indian, Sioux or Crow;
> Little frosty Eskimo;
> Little Turk or Japanee;
> O! don't you wish that you were me?

America could no longer have a privileged white class at the expense of minorities. We WASPs may once have run the nation, but that time was passing. Life in America would be better for most people, if not all.

Even so, I think now with affection of the old-fashioned Richmond I discovered in the 1940s. I was glad to be back in Virginia, enjoying its WASPs and its tomahtoes. As Aunt Lucy Durham used to say on West End Avenue, "Richmond is a town of gentle people." Virginia, too.

WASPs–gentle WASPs. May they continue to stay aloft in a changing world.

The motion of my blood no longer keeps time with the tumult of the world. It leads me to seek for happiness in the lap and love of my family, in the society of my neighbors and books, in the wholesome occupations of my farms and my affairs, in an interest or affection in every bud that opens, every breath that blows around me . . .

Thomas Jefferson to James Madison, 1793

Epilogue

NOW, in 1996, I can't believe all that happened more than a half century ago.

Most of the people I've mentioned here have "gone to their reward," as the *Prayer Book* says. After I married Betsy Gayle in Richmond in 1946, we had twin daughters and a son, and I reluctantly gave up the *Times-Dispatch* to move to Williamsburg to join the Rockefeller-endowed Restoration. In 1954 the Commonwealth of Virginia chose me to organize and direct the 1957 celebration of America's 350 years of British settlement. Out of that grew museums at Jamestown and Yorktown, which I helped create for the Jamestown-Yorktown Foundation.

I retired in 1980 in Williamsburg to a life of writing and travel and grandchildren.

Many aspects of Richmond have changed since the 1940s. The afternoon *News Leader* ceased publication, done in by TV newscasting. Colgate Darden, Jr., was succeeded as governor in 1946 by Bill Tuck. The Virginia Historical Society moved from the Stewart-Lee house downtown to Battle Abbey on the Boulevard, and Richmond's westward movement desolated its old downtown hub of commerce. Interstate highways remade the city.

My cousin Gus Edwards, whose wedding I mention, went to war and became a major general. Mary Tyler Cheek, Douglas Freeman's daughter whom I mentioned as Mrs. Leslie Cheek, Jr., married after Leslie's death Dr. John McClenahan. Similarly, Maria Williams Sheerin, mentioned as the widow of the Reverend Charles Sheerin, married again and became before her death Mrs. John Minor of Washington.

I appreciate the generosity of friends who have told me the stories which help make Virginia Waspish, and I hope I may collect others. I have acknowledged most sources, both living and dead, elsewhere in these pages.

Most important of all, Virginia and the rest of the nation finally righted the terrible wrong of racial segregation. After years of contention the United States after 1954 began to implement the Supreme Court's epic decision.

I am proud of the role the *Times-Dispatch* played under Virginius Dabney and the *News Leader* under Douglas Freeman. I am happy to have been in Richmond in those exciting days.

Acknowledgments

I WOULD LIKE to acknowledge that the impetus for this book came from Edith McMurran (Mrs. Lewis McMurran, Jr.) of Newport News and from Lee and George Cochran of Staunton. I received encouragement along the way, from my wife, Betsy; from Dorothy Cowardin Gibson (Mrs. Ross Gibson of Richmond); and Kelso Alsop Everett (Mrs. Charles Everett), of Wilmington, Delaware.

I received stories and other material from the following friends, both living and dead:

Dr. Robert Finley Gayle, Jr., Paul Murphy, Mary Blair Scott Valentine (Mrs. Stuart Valentine), Edith Reed Funsten (Mrs. Herbert Funsten), Dr. John Alexander, Barry Bingham, Helena Lefroy Caperton (Mrs. Arthur Caperton), Paul Saunier, Corbin Old, Edith Lindeman Calisch (Mrs. Woolner Calisch), Mary Tyler McClenahan (Mrs. John McClenahan), Agnes Moyler Jones (Mrs. Decatur Jones), Willis Shell, James Latimer, Overton Jones, Willis Lathrop Starbuck (Mrs. Bayard G. Starbuck), Mrs. Virginia Wellford Jones, Eda Carter Williams (Mrs. Walter Williams), Margaret Williams McElroy (Mrs. John McElroy), Vaughan Scott (Mrs. Walter Scott), Susan Carter Williams (Mrs. Fielding Williams), Dr. Armistead Dandridge Williams, Mate Branch Converse (Mrs. Henry Converse), Hartwell Reed, Charles Larus Reed.

Maria Williams Minor (Mrs. John Minor), Eva Wise Mills, David Tennant Bryan, John Stewart Bryan, Joseph Bryan III, Granville Valentine, Major Murray Forbes Bayliss, RAF, Ennolls Stephens, John Garland Pollard IV, Betty Cocke Pollard (Mrs. Charles Pollard), Senator William A. Wright, William Lashley, Randolph Dashiell Rouse, Rebecca Yancey Williams (Mrs. John Bell Williams), Jane Hutcheson Talley (Mrs. Richard Talley), Frank Dementi, Rose Kauffman Banks, Marshall Penick Wiltshire (Mrs. George Wiltshire), Willis Shell, Jr., John Cole Gayle, and Mrs. Eda Williams Martin.

I am greatly indebted to Jacqueline Danner Taylor (Mrs. Don Taylor), who typed the manuscript and made many helpful suggestions.

I especially appreciate the kindness of friends in reading the manuscript and making editorial suggestions. They are Mary Tyler McClenahan (Mrs. John McClenahan), Virginia Wellford Jones, Dorothy Cowardin Gibson (Mrs. Ross Shackelford Gibson), James Latimer, and especially my wife, whose lifetime immersion in Richmond gave me access to many of the people and occasions I have described.

For help with illustrations, I am indebted to the Association for the Preservation of Virginia Antiquities; Jack Davis and Mrs. Nancy Coram of the Newport News *Daily Press*; D. Tennant Bryan, Ms. Joanne Slough, and Ms. Kathy Albers of the *Richmond Times-Dispatch*; Nolan Yelich and Ms. Petie Bogen-Garrett of the Library of Virginia; Mrs. Susan Bruno of the *Virginia Gazette*; and Ms. Ann Marie Price of the Virginia Historical Society.

Parke Rouse, Jr.
Williamsburg, Virginia

Bibliography

BAGBY, GEORGE W. *The Old Virginia Gentleman and Other Sketches*. New York: Scribner's, 1910.

BRYAN, JOHN STEWART. *Joseph Bryan, His Times, His Family and His Friends*. Richmond: Whittet and Shepperson, 1935.

CABELL, JAMES BRANCH. *Let Me Lie*. New York: Farrar, Straus, 1947.

CABELL, JAMES BRANCH. *As I Remember It*. New York: McBride, 1955.

CHESTNUT, MARY BOYKIN. *A Diary from Dixie*. Ed. Ben Ames Williams. Boston: Houghton Mifflin, 1949.

DABNEY, VIRGINIUS. *Richmond, The Story of a City*. Garden City: Doubleday, 1976.

DABNEY, VIRGINIUS. *Virginia: The New Dominion*. Garden City: Doubleday, 1971.

DOWDEY, CLIFFORD. *Experiment in Rebellion*. Garden City: Doubleday, 1946.

FREEMAN, DOUGLAS S. *R. E. Lee*. 4 vols. New York: Scribner, 1934–1935.

FREEMAN, DOUGLAS S. *The South to Posterity*. New York: Scribner, 1939.

FREEMAN, DOUGLAS S. *Lee's Lieutenants*. Vol. III. New York: Scribner, 1944.

FREEMAN, ANN HOBSON. *The Style of a Law Firm: Eight Gentlemen from Virginia*. Chapel Hill: Algonquin Books, 1989.

MORTON, RICHARD L. *Colonial Virginia*. 2 vols. Chapel Hill: Univ. of North Carolina Press, 1960.

Of Two Virginia Gentlemen and Their McGuire's University School. Richmond: Carmine Graphics, 1972.

SCOTT, MARY WINGFIELD. *Houses of Old Richmond*. Richmond: Valentine Museum, 1941.

SCOTT, MARY WINGFIELD. *Old Richmond Neighborhoods*. Richmond: Whittet and Shepperson, 1950.

SYKES, CHRISTOPHER. *Nancy, The Life of Lady Astor*. New York: Harper, 1972.

Index

B

C

D

G

H

I

J

K

N

O

P

Q

R

S

T

U

V

Y

Z